WHAT Color IS YOUR God?

WHAT Color IS YOUR God?

David Ireland

IMPACT PUBLISHING HOUSE

VERONA, NEW JERSEY

© 2000 by David Ireland

IMPACT Publishing House
96 Pompton Ave.
Verona, New Jersey, U.S.A. 07044
www.impactministry.org

ISBN 0-9627907-3-7
Printed in the United States of America
LC 00-100990

Library of Congress Cataloging-in Publishing Data

Ireland, David, 1961—
What Color Is Your God? / David Ireland.
     p.   cm.
     Includes bibliographical references.
     ISBN 0-9627907-3-7
     1. What Color Is Your God?—United States.
     I. Title.
        2000

Unless otherwise indicated, Scripture references are taken from the HOLY BIBLE, NEW INTERNATIONAL VERSION®. NIV®

Copyright© 1973, 1978, 1984 by International Bible Society. Used by permission of Zondervan Bible Publishers. All rights reserved.

Scripture quotations marked KJV are taken from the King James Version of the Bible.

Scripture quotations marked NAS are taken from the New American Standard Bible. Copyright. The Lockman Foundation 1960, 1962. 1971, 1972, 1973, 1975, 1977. Used by permission.

For current information about all releases from Impact Publishing House, visit our web site: www.impactministry.org.

Dedication

This book is dedicated to my children, Danielle and Jessica. Through the encouragement of the sacred Scriptures, I have endeavored to leave a spiritual legacy to your generation, particularly in the area of modeling a multicultural lifestyle. Your many positive questions and comments on the subject of cultural diversity forecast a world with less racial tension.

This book is also dedicated to Cinda Gaskin, my research editor, for her tireless effort in reviewing the manuscript.

Also by David Ireland

Unlocking the Supernatural

Activating the Gifts of the Holy Spirit

Failure Is Written In Pencil

Contents

INTRODUCTION

When asked what is America's greatest conflict, Dr. Billy Graham answered "prejudice and racism." Both within and without the church, many people are living in perilous denial of prejudice and racism, with no biblical answers to this current social ill. If people don't understand what the Bible has to say about the everyday problems people face in the real world, they will be forced to turn to the world for answers. Unfortunately, worldly solutions don't have redemptive qualities or moral values worth passing on to the next generation. For this reason, *in a divided society, the church must model unity.*

In one of the most memorable speeches of the twentieth century, "I Have a Dream," Dr. Martin Luther King, Jr. spoke of a future society where his children "would not be judged by the color of their skin but by the content of their character." King's cry for justice and racial equality articulated the definition of a good society—one in which the true richness of multiculturalism would be understood and practiced. Multiculturalism is a respect for diversity, concern for various cultural groups, provision of equal opportunities, and a just balance of power among the many groups that constitute the United States. This meaning forms a framework of what society would look like under ideal conditions of cross-cultural relations. In order to achieve a truly multicultural society, the church must embody the biblical teaching of being our brother's keeper (Gen. 4:9). Providing care and compassion to the global community of Christians and non-Christians alike carries out this mandate. The apostle Paul clearly instructs Christians, *"As we have opportunity, let us do good to all people, especially to those who belong to the family of believers"* (Gal. 6:10). The Scriptures direct the church to perform practical acts of love to all kinds of people, albeit, this exemplary behavior should first be shown to the Christian community.

Character, community, and culture are the basic elements of human interaction needed to achieve the good society. The good society, is the revitalization of five key areas: marketplace ethics, education, social movements, family, and faith.[1] In order to attain this noble objective, the Christian community must demonstrate and uphold the commandment: *"'Love the Lord your God with all your heart and with all your soul and with all your strength and with all your mind'; and, 'Love your neighbor as yourself'"* (Luke 10:27).

The Bible uses two metaphors to describe Christians who practice their faith on a societal level; these are salt and light (Matt. 5:13–16). Salt denotes a preservative, and light represents goodness and righteousness. Jesus used these terms to describe the type of lasting positive change that society should undergo when individuals set out to make a contribution within their sphere of influence. Integrating this directive of the gospel for Christians to become agents of change (salt and light) would demonstrate the fundamental principles of faith, compassion, equality, jurisdictional authority, and the love Jesus prescribed for mankind. If we are to see multiculturalism and individual multicultural lifestyles actualized in the United States, such pivotal institutions as business and economics, the family, and the church must be reshaped.

Sectors of our society support a more secularized understanding of multiculturalism, upholding the equality of the gay life, different experiences, perspectives, and truths. The preferred definition of multiculturalism, which addresses the overall good of society, indicates that all cultures (not sexual orientations) are of equal importance. When ethnic inclusion is not promoted for the good of society, tolerance is introduced as the medicine for ailing intercultural relationships. *Tolerance* is the unbiased acceptance of others, their values, rights, freedoms, and perspectives.

The term *political correctness* has been integrated into the vocabulary of mainstream American society to prevent intolerance. The term is intended "to enforce a uniform standard of tolerance, regardless of race, gender, cultural background or sexual orientation."[2] The problem with this concept is that it parallels incongruent entities, such as sexual orientation and cultural equality. This interpretation of society labels a person as "intolerant" and "politically incorrect" if he does not accept and even approve of immoral behavior. This dilemma in definition and practice begs the question: *How can Christians introduce lasting societal change?*

The Christian's responsibility is to reestablish the definition of multiculturalism, so that it parallels the original intent of Dr. King's "I Have a Dream speech". This approach leaves no room for the Christian community to take on isolationistic perspectives with regard to race relations. Christians must be on the forefront of the battle because of the need to preserve human dignity and practice biblical justice (Matt. 23:23; Gal. 6:10). Two principles germane to effective cross-cultural interaction are found in this book: First, cross-cultural communication can be learned; second, true love must be at the heart of inclusion.

Christian societal involvement is not a passive function steeped in pietistic behavior. Neither is Christian societal reform supposed to illicit radical, politicized actions to achieve our desired outcome. Although a number of the proponents of the Religious Right use a biblically based approach to social reform, they sometimes misconstrue the legislative process as a continuum of biblical Christianity and view the Republican Party as God's representatives. The problem with this philosophy, according to Edward Dobson, a board member of the Moral Majority, is that the situation tends towards intolerance."[3] Ralph Reed, president of the Christian Coalition, noted in a recent forum on race that "the legacy of Jim Crow segregation and racism that the white evangelical community still carries is like an albatross, and there is a chasm of a very painful history that we've still got to bridge."[4] Reformation of the American family and multiculturalism can occur effectively on a grass roots level only through personal instruction and mentoring.

When the church's philosophy is "Churches are here to help people," and not "people are here to help churches," a more intentional approach to societal reform must be adopted by various congregations. The church belongs to all members, and bringing reform to the congregation and ultimately to the community requires that the organizational culture of the church move toward ethnic inclusion. Recognizing the gifts of all believers and establishing intentional leadership development programs will equip and encourage the various ethnic constituencies to do the work of ministry. An organizational culture of love is created and fostered by the congregation as it intentionally reaches out to its community. I believe that this mindset toward inclusion requires that the congregation participate in four areas: 1) meeting the needs of the people; 2) focusing on worship and education; 3) practicing evangelism; and, 4) committing to hard work.

As Christians, we cannot behave like ostriches, burying our heads in holes and expect the good society to be actualized apart from our involvement. We have a responsibility, a moral one, to exemplify racial reconciliation in the spheres of business and economics, the family, and the church. I cannot help but think that if we were equally committed to fulfilling the mandate to love our neighbors, the good society would not be simply an ideal place; it would be manifested in our midst. The church has a biblical mandate to establish reconciliation work-shops, conferences, and sensitivity training for its members in order to promote unity in God's house. And, in a divided society, the church must model unity.

Chapter 1

THE MISSION OF THE MARKETPLACE

W hen God touches your life, it should come as no surprise that He may be launching you in a new direction, with a new purpose that you never before imagined. I had become an atheist by the time I was a teenager. As a college student, I frequently went out of my way to antagonize Christians. When I first went to church, a number of students thought I had simply come to cause trouble. Following my conversion at age twenty, I became a person who would boldly share his faith with anyone who would listen. But that wasn't the only surprising turn God had in store for me.

Growing up, I was undoubtedly influenced by the racial and prejudicial attitudes of those in my neighborhood. But somewhere along the way, I made a decision to not allow the racist perceptions of others to influence my life. Throughout high school, college, and as I began my career, I had no problem developing interracial friendships. I felt comfortable with all types of people. Consequently, there was no driving passion within me regarding racial reconciliation. But God had a special calling for me in this area.

Soon after I became a Christian, I began to notice how multicultural the world was becoming and how monocultural the church was remaining. I couldn't ignore the fact that Koreans mainly worshipped at Korean churches, whites mainly worshipped at white churches, African-americans mainly worshipped at African-American churches, and so on. Nevertheless, I couldn't fathom the dynamics and difficulties of the various groups worshipping together as a single, relationally based expression of the church.

At that time, my wife, Marlinda, and I were living in Irvington, New Jersey. It was there that a burden began to grow in my heart. In those days, I often experienced the strongest spiritual impressions at the grocery store in our neighborhood.

It seemed as if every type of person from every nation on earth was represented at our grocery store, any time of the day you showed up. The store had special sections with Indian, Thai, and other ethnic foods. Watching the people of different races standing together in the checkout lines caused my heart to be moved profoundly. But getting teary-eyed while standing in the checkout line is both embarrassing and hard to explain. Why can't it be like this in church? I thought. The need for the gospel and the desire to worship are as universal as our common need for food.

But it seemed to me that the typical local church was posturing itself in a way that was more exclusive than inclusive. This observation caused me to become more aware of my own superstitions, attitudes, and prejudices.

The logical side of me—the side that used to do *all* the talking before I came to Christ—said, *Every group has its own church, where the members can feel free to worship among their own cultural, social, and racial peers.* That seemed reasonable, but I just couldn't get away from what I felt when I saw the diverse groups of people congregating in the malls, grocery stores, and other public places.

Now I realize that it was the Holy Spirit speaking to my heart through the ordinary occurrences of my life. And obedience to His voice was really the beginning of Christ Church, which today is a thriving congregation representing more than twenty-five nationalities.

In its fledgling state, our church was monoracial and did not model the multicultural world. Soon, the vision that God had given me began to take form as the Holy Spirit drew other ethnic groups into our small fellowship.

Although the ministry topics were typical for an evangelical church, I worked hard to present messages that were not culturally limiting. Early on in my ministry I realized that all people have the same needs. Once you get past the differences in skin color and hair texture, you realize that our basic need of a sense of self-worth and personal fulfillment is the same. The challenge in building relationships along lines of diversity is more than simply *practicing* equity; it involves communicating the *perception* of equity.

People in different cultural groups often see the world through their own cultural lens. Consequently, *perspective* is more concrete than fact or reality. In growing a multicultural congregation, we had to learn to listen to one another's perspectives, even though many had distorted viewpoints that skewed their perception of reality. Trust had to be developed so that the business of the kingdom (winning souls and making disciples) would be our primary focus.

During those formative years, one of the biggest challenges I faced was dealing with people who wanted to redirect the mission of the church. Whenever they encountered someone from their own ethnic group who had an effective ministry, they felt that the church should elevate this person and move to "their" part of town, to reach "their people." Actually, we were never really able to choose the neighborhood in which we met. We met wherever we could find a facility. As a young church, we met in various rented facilities for worship. Twice we were asked to leave with very little notice because a landlord felt threatened by our growth and the multicultural makeup of our congregation. As God would have it, we always seemed to end up in either an interracial or a predominately white community.

Though no one actually came out and said that our church should be monoracial, some people were very intent that the church reflect *their culture* alone. Their vision was for the church to become exclusive, but I knew that this was not the desire of God's heart. Everything about God's heart cries to include all of the people who have walked through the doors of salvation opened by Christ.

Many times I got an earful of opinions about how my responsibility was first and foremost to my own ethnic group. In truth, I didn't have a solid scriptural answer to refute these arguments. I was simply responding to the burden that had begun in a grocery store and was now growing into a unique church.

Several years ago at a conference of Christian college students, the first session opened with a processional. As those in attendance worshipped the Lord, all the international students marched down the aisles and around the convention center, each carrying his or her nation's flag. It looked very similar to the opening ceremonies at the Olympic Games. Some nations had large groups of students following the flag bearers, waving their hands and praising God. Other groups were smaller. And then there were the students who marched alone, carrying their flags as the sole representatives of their countries. The music leader continued to sing songs about all the nations bowing before the Lord Jesus Christ. It wasn't long before most of the people were on their knees, weeping and worshipping the King of Kings. There was something about that processional, with all the nations presenting themselves before the throne, that touched us very deeply.

In ancient times, when a king subdued another nation, he would have men and women brought from that nation to serve in his court. Such was the case with Daniel (Dan. 1:19) and Nehemiah, who served King Artaxerxes (Neh. 2:1). The purpose was to demonstrate to all who entered the king's court that he was a great king, a "king of kings," so to speak, who had conquered many nations.

It is the purpose and passion of the Father to fully exalt and glorify the Son in all the earth. Psalm 86:9 tells us, *"All the nations you have made will come and worship before you, O Lord."* The worship that is foretold in Psalm 86 is pictured in the Revelation of John:

> [9]*After this I looked and there before me was a great multitude that no one could count, from every nation, tribe, people and language, standing before the throne and in front of the Lamb. They were wearing white robes and were holding palm branches in their hands.* [10]*And they cried out in a loud voice: "Salvation belongs to our God, who sits on the throne, and to the Lamb."* (Rev. 7:9–10)

The same kind of multinational worship is referred to in a similar passage elsewhere in Revelation, depicting a heavenly model of the church. The four living creatures and the twenty-four elders fall down before the throne and worship the Lamb with this song:

> [9]*"You are worthy...because you were slain, and with your blood you purchased men for God from every tribe and language and people and nation.* [10]*You have made them to be a kingdom and priests to serve our God, and they will reign on the earth."* (Rev. 5:9–10)

When all nations worship and bow before Him, the character and intensity of worship rises to its highest level. Christ is, in that place, exalted as the King of Kings and Lord of Lords. Worship from an exclusive group certainly glorifies God, but the potential impact of witness and worship is diminished. The greatest witness to His sacrifice is when people from every tribe, tongue, and nation are brought into the kingdom of God. That's why diversity is the character of the kingdom—because it is for the greatest glory of the Son. Again, the passion of the Father is to exalt the Son as King of all nations. That is the motivation behind every aspect of God's plan and purpose. It is also His desire to replicate that passion in each of His children.

What was it that created such a burden in my heart as I watched the nations flow into the market? What brought those at the conference to their knees? I believe it was the Holy Spirit bearing witness to the purpose of God. When we behold something that resembles what the kingdom of God is really like, even in a dim image, the Spirit leaps within us. The glimpse of the kingdom in the book of Revelation is a picture of what the church on earth should be like. That's what Jesus taught us to pray for—that the kingdom would come on earth as it is in heaven (Matt. 6:9–13).

Every so often people would leave our church because they disagreed with one thing or another. Occasionally, the topics of tolerance and accommodation of various cultural expressions of worship, prayer, and preaching would emerge. Those who saw the diversity of people and various cultural expressions of worship merely as issues of tolerance *completely* missed the point. Imagine that someone at the student conference had demanded that all the other nations just hurry up and get out of the way so that he could see his own nation's flag!

A person sensitive to the heart of God rejoices in diversity because it exalts Jesus as King of Kings and Lord of Lords. It is a reflection of what's going on in heaven. Those who are impatiently tapping their feet, perhaps congratulating themselves for their tolerance, have their minds and hearts set on something other than the agenda of the kingdom.

As the church grew, with wonderful people being saved and added, I'd occasionally receive letters from people who did not want to continue at Christ Church because the church wasn't Afro-centric enough. Others left because it was too Afro-centric, or too Anglo-centric, or because it centered on something other than what they preferred.

It always pains a pastor when someone leaves the church, but as these people left I discovered a truth I'd needed for four years. I found that in being Christ-centered, I could not be racially or culturally centered any more than I could be self-centered or money-centered. This didn't mean that I should ignore my own culture, history, and heritage; neither was I expecting that of the people in my church. But I realized that as Christians, we cannot allow the consciousness of culture to remain at the center of our lives, faith, and worship.

To live out the full meaning of the kingdom, a passion for Christ and His kingdom has to occupy that place of preeminence. I finally had a legitimate answer to the question I'd been struggling with. When He said, *"Therefore go and make disciples of all nations"* (Matt. 28:19), Christ commissioned me to be a cultural ambassador, heralding the message of salvation to all nationalities. The word *nation* is the Greek word *ethnos*, which is where the English word *ethnic* is derived. This means that Jesus commissions the church to make disciples of every ethnic group. It was an incredible revelation to discover that if I were to become ethnocentric, I could not live a life that is Christocentric.

When a Christian is not Christ-centered, there is idolatry at work somewhere. Christocentrism must be the gravitational force which holds all the components of one's life in place. If I become exclusive to one

21

tribe, tongue, people, or nation, then I'm no longer walking in step with Christ, and I'm no longer following the Great Commission. I can be ethno-*conscious* and remain Christ-centered, but not ethnocentric.

God made us what we are, and everything He made is good. Thus, the conscious knowledge of one's heritage is supported in the teachings of the apostle Paul, who recorded in Scripture that he was *"circumcised on the eighth day, of the people of Israel, of the tribe of Benjamin, a Hebrew of Hebrews; in regard to the law, a Pharisee"* (Phil. 3:5). But while Paul was keenly conscious of his ethnicity, he also admonished us not to put our confidence in the flesh (Phil. 3:3–4).

THE END OF RECONCILIATION

You might say that I "backed into" the ministry of reconciliation. The reconciliation movement has been growing and gaining momentum over the last few years in the U.S. and overseas. At conferences and meetings from Washington, D.C., to Johannesburg, South Africa, Christians have been forging initiatives to address the guilt and pain resulting from generations of offenses. While I applaud those efforts, I can't help but ask what happens when everyone goes home from these events? After people are forgiven and healed, then what? Do they really go out and make an effort to build relationships with individuals from other racial and ethnic groups? Does the racial and ethnic makeup of their close friendships change? When repentance and reconciliation are the main events at denominational conventions, is this evidenced by a new ethnic diversity in local congregations?

I'm not questioning the sincerity of any of these efforts. For many people, it required a lot of prayer and soul-searching to take those initial reconciliatory steps. But my observation is that if the upshot of these efforts is not the formation of new relationships and a greater congregational diversity, then the vision is shortsighted and does not line up with the standard of the kingdom presented in Scripture.

The burden God put on my heart was to build a church that would model what the kingdom of God is to look like—His kingdom coming on earth, as it is in heaven. That means worshipping and fellowshipping with *all kinds* of people around the throne of grace. You see, what drives me primarily is the passion to exalt Christ and to establish His visible kingdom. I also have a great desire to build real, not token, relationships with every one of my true brothers and sisters in Christ. But to accomplish either of these goals in my church means that we all will have to deal with past offenses. In many cases, the list of hurts and offenses is very long and very old. Reconciliation is indeed the first step, but if that's all that takes place, we will never get around to accomplishing the burden of the Father's heart. So then, the purpose or end of reconciliation is kingdom diversity on earth, even as it is in heaven.

The highest expression of worship, the most strategic efforts in spiritual warfare, and the most mature expressions of God's kingdom through the church cannot be approached without dealing with man's resistance to diversity in the light of God's express desire for it.

This book is, naturally, a reflection of what my Lord has graciously placed in my heart as a personal mission. It is the joyful outworking of the steps one must take to become a cultural ambassador. My goal in writing this book is not to add to the increasing amount of literature that simply points to the problem of prejudice both inside and outside the church. Rather, the aim is to equip the church to provoke its constituency to greater works of love.

I address the issues of prejudice, which leads to racism, and reconciliation, which leads to restoration. But every time and in every setting in which I talk about these things, my intention is to build Christ's kingdom through the construction of local Christian models of diversity. Though I am concerned with societal reform, I am consumed with what I understand to be the Holy Spirit's desire to prepare the church as the bride of Christ who has made herself ready for His coming. The aim of this book is not to rehearse the age-old problems of racism. Rather, my goal is to offer workable solutions for modeling diversity.

Chapter 2

DIVERSITY: THE NATURE OF THE KINGDOM

P eople streamed out of Christ Church after the benediction. For many the next stop was a local restaurant. Two families that had grown fond of each other's company made arrangements to meet for brunch at a nearby diner. One family was white with no children, and the other family was black with two toddlers. As they recounted the story to me, they said, "Pastor, you should have seen the stares and double takes we got from the other patrons in the restaurant as we walked in." The white man was holding one of the toddlers in his arms, and his wife was holding the other African-American toddler in her arms. The children's parents were still parking their car. Finally, after the parents walked into the diner and took their seats at the table, the patrons' minds were put at ease because the racial puzzle was solved.

In the late 1980s a South African woman who had immigrated to the United States under the status of political asylum began attending our church. Her government back home was still operating under the oppressive rule of apartheid. During worship she was astonished as she tried to understand how whites and blacks were able to worship God under the same roof. Far more startling to her was when two of the pastors, one white and the other black, took turns addressing the congregation. After the sermon, she commented that she never had imagined she would see the day when various races would worship freely together. Tears streamed down her face as she described her feelings. "We strive to model the diversity within the kingdom of God," I said as I gave her a hug. It has been said that a picture is worth a thousand words. How true this was for this dear lady from South Africa. All the rhetoric of reconciliation and restitution meant little without the visible demonstration of a social model.

A NEW WAY OF THINKING

Every now and then you hear a new idea that causes you to reconsider your previous conclusions. Although "paradigm shift" is a relatively new buzzword, the process is as old as dirt. For example, in the scientific world the greatest eye-opener of all time was the simple theory of Nicolaus Copernicus (1473–1543), that the earth turns on its axis and at the same time orbits the sun. This concept seems obvious to us in the twenty-first century, but this was not the case in the early sixteenth century.

For centuries before Copernicus, all astronomers had gazed into the heavens with the assumption that the world stood fixed and still in space, while the sun and stars whirled around it. They found it inconceivable that the earth, which seemed to be still, was moving, and the stars, which seemed to be moving, were relatively fixed in the sky. In Copernicus' day, the greatest scientific minds on earth had created complex models to explain the movement of heavenly bodies "circling the earth" every day. The Copernican Revolution simply overturned the apple cart of scientific knowledge. It forced every scientist to rethink all the old assumptions, and it birthed an entirely new understanding of an immense universe—one in which the earth was not the center.

The spiritual and theological counterpart of the Copernican Revolution was the coming of Jesus. Christ forced everyone, particularly His followers, to radically reexamine their expectations and understanding of the kingdom. What one believes about the kingdom of God is foundational because it shapes all of our other beliefs. It also affects how we expect God's kingdom to be practically worked out in our churches and in our everyday lives. For instance, the people in New Testament times, including the followers of Jesus, had a rigid understanding of what the kingdom of God would look like. Simply put, they thought the Messiah would come on the scene, raise up a great following, and with the help of some extraordinary divine intervention, kick out the occupying Roman Army. He would then take his seat on the throne of his ancestor, King David, and rule on the earth.

A misconception of the kingdom caused many to miss the Messiah when He came. It caused those who did recognize Him to misunderstand the nature and purpose of the kingdom. Most of the Pharisees and priests, and even one of Jesus' twelve disciples, opposed the purpose of God because they inaccurately perceived the nature of the kingdom. After the resurrection and ascension, even the apostles had to rethink their understanding of a kingdom that was not at all what they expected it to be. On the day of Pentecost, Peter preached about the resurrection and ascension of Jesus, explaining how this fulfilled the prophecies of the Messiah, who would ascend to the throne of David. How different was this perception from that of the disciples who, until the end, interpreted the kingdom in terms of an earthly rule.

Jesus taught about many aspects of the kingdom of God. The great revelation that changed how I practiced my faith and developed my vision for the church was that diversity is a fundamental characteristic of the kingdom. As a young Christian, when I led people to Christ through personal evangelism, I often struggled with what church to recommend to them. Race was a significant factor. Every church did not accommodate all types of people. Jesus died for everyone, yet the local churches did not receive all those for whom He died. I was challenged by the Holy Spirit to help bring reformation to the churches within my sphere of influence. My plea to them was that the church must reflect the kingdom to which it belongs.

As I continued to study the Bible and think about the dynamics of diversity in the kingdom of God, I was drawn to take another look at familiar passages of Scripture in light of my new understanding. Here are a few simple observations about the kingdom.

1. The Nature of the Kingdom is Inclusion, Not Exclusion.

Several years ago our church decided to reach out to a number of families that were experiencing some financial misfortune during the Christmas season. We approached a local school board and were given a list of families that could use some cheering up. We donated fruit baskets, toys, and other holiday goodies. Later, we invited the families to a gala event and presented Christ to all who came. To our delight, many people made decisions for Christ. But within a few weeks we noticed that the single mothers were no longer attending our church and would not return our telephone calls. One mom finally voiced the reason why she had dropped out. She said she did not feel a sense of belonging at our church. As far as she could see, none of the young ladies in the church were in her social category. None were single with children. The other single ladies in the church were either in college, married, or single professionals in the work force.

Frankly, I am embarrassed to share that these new converts did not feel a sense of inclusion because we were not sensitive to their predicament. Consequently, they felt that they didn't belong in our church community. We were not aware of their internal struggles with social alienation or that we were excluding them. Whether exclusion is a conscious act or an unconscious one, it's still very painful.

This experience supports the church growth statisticians' assertions about the role of friendship in maintaining low dropout rates for new church members. In his doctoral dissertation, Flavil Yeakley, a church growth researcher, commented, "When a person has no meaningful personal contacts with the congregation in the process of his conversion, he is likely to feel no meaningful sense of identification with the congregation after his conversion and is therefore likely to drop out."[1] This was indeed the case in our evangelistic outreach. It was also true that we needed to create an inclusive atmosphere for these young ladies.

The Pharisees understood the kingdom to be exclusive, open only to people like them. While eating at the house of a prominent Pharisee, one of those at the table with Jesus said to Him, *"Blessed is everyone who shall eat bread in the kingdom of God!"* (Luke 14:15 NAS). Jesus responded by telling the story of a man who had prepared a banquet and invited many of his friends. However, those who were initially invited refused to come. Jesus continued:

[21] *"The servant came back and reported this to his master. Then the owner of the house became angry and ordered his servant, 'Go out quickly into the streets and alleys of the town and bring in the poor, the crippled, the blind and the lame.' [22] 'Sir,' the servant said, 'what you ordered has been*

done, but there is still room.' [23]*Then the master told his servant, 'Go out to the roads and country lanes and make them come in, so that my house will be full.'"*

(Luke 14:21–23)

God doesn't want us to simply "tolerate" diversity. His heart is that we compel all kinds of people to come into His kingdom. I'm not suggesting that our evangelistic efforts be loose and unfocused. Rather, my views regarding targeted evangelism are the same as those of many pastors of thriving evangelism-based congregations. Rick Warren, who pastors a congregation of ten thousand members, writes, "When we plan an evangelistic effort, we always have a specific target in mind. The Bible determines our message, but our target determines when, where, and how we communicate it."[2]

While I agree that we should brainstorm and prayerfully create specific methods to reach specific groups of people, my concern is that the church remain connected with the inclusive focus of the Great Commission. Many congregations, in an attempt to grow via evangelism, target specific groups and ignore everyone else in their community. This is not true, Bible-centered evangelism. Although we target specific groups via a specific model, we must not target one group exclusively. This approach would ignore the Great Commission and result in a completely monoracial church.

When I was in seminary, one of my class projects was to evaluate the impact of two local churches on a community. Since my major was Urban Ministry, I decided to gather my research data from Corona, Queens, a small urban community located outside New York City. Corona is a unique place. Within its four square miles, more than 104 different languages are spoken. Each of the two churches I visited was

Evangelical and had five hundred to seven hundred congregants. But the dynamics of the two congregations were exactly the opposite of one another. One church was totally monoracial; the other was composed of people of every hue imaginable. The latter church resembled the United Nations, while the former reminded me of a private meeting of an exclusive fraternity.

Both churches preached evangelism, yet only one represented the composition of its community. I concluded that the attitude held by the monoracial church was that the people they reached for Christ must conform to their monolithic "style" of ministry. *We refuse to change!* was the sentiment they expressed nonverbally. Conversely, the congregation that modeled diversity was continually making adjustments to accommodate the different ethnic groups they felt God wanted them to reach for Christ.

2. The Holy Spirit is Himself the Author of Diversity in the Church.

In 1 Corinthians 12, the apostle Paul exhorted the Corinthian church regarding spiritual gifts, writing:

> [4]*There are different kinds of gifts, but the same Spirit.* [5]*There are different kinds of service, but the same Lord.* [6]*There are different kinds of working, but the same God works all of them in all men.* [7]*Now to each one the manifestation of the Spirit is given for the common good....*[11]*All these are the work of one and the same Spirit, and he gives them to each one, just as He determines.* (1 Cor. 12:4–7, 11)

Variety in the church is not an accident; it is God's express intention. Church leaders must recognize the diversity of spiritual gifts

(1 Cor. 12), ministry callings (Eph. 4), and motivations for service (Rom. 12) of the people within their congregations. They also need to recognize that God Himself is the one who orchestrates diversity by placing certain people in a particular local church. Paul addressed this need, writing, *"But in fact God has arranged the parts in the body, every one of them, just as he wanted them to be"* (1 Cor. 12:18). Robert Webber, noted author on worship, writes, "[The church] is not an aggregate of individuals, but a corporate body of people who constitute a unique society within the societies of the world."[3] Thus, we understand that God's placement of people is neither random nor haphazard. It is with purpose and intention. Conversely, there are people whom God does not place in certain churches because He knows they would not receive the love, attention, and recognition He desires for them.

God's will is to sovereignly gather and place a diversity of ethnic and racial people-groups within His body to demonstrate to the world what His kingdom is like. In the middle of his discussion of the diversity of gifts, Paul wrote:

> [12]*The body is a unit, though it is made up of many parts; and though all its parts are many, they form one body. So it is with Christ.* [13]*For we were all baptized by one Spirit into one body—whether Jews or Greeks, slave or free—and we were all given the one Spirit to drink.* (1 Cor. 12:12–13)

The relationships between Jews, Gentiles, slaves, and freemen represented the most significant cultural stress points of first-century Palestinian society. Paul indicated not only that God distributes a variety of spiritual gifts to benefit the church, but that the Holy Spirit Himself baptizes people from every ethnic, cultural, economic, social, and racial group into one body. Throughout most of the New Testament, there is the constant apostolic reminder that the church cannot be divided or segregated into economic, cultural, or racial distinctions. We have been made one in Christ.

God includes all people from every conceivable background in the church. People's lives are shaped by the culture and environment from which they come. Various cultural and ethnic groups bring a passion to worship, prayer, and evangelism. Others have been graced with a quiet spirit that enables them to seek the depths of God through meditation and prayer. For instance, the church worldwide has learned a great deal about prayer from the Korean Christians. David Yongii Cho's frequent reference in his books to Prayer Mountain, a retreat site dedicated exclusively for prayer, has provoked many Christians to make prayer a greater priority in their lives.

While there is not strong biblical support for the premise that each race has inherent gifts that are unique to that group, I can support theologically the idea that our experiences (some unique to each race) enable us to add a dimension of perspective, value, and sensitivity to the body of Christ, that may not otherwise have been gained.

The twelve tribes of Israel each had different specialties due to the vocational, environmental, or spiritual emphases of their predecessors. The priesthood came from the Levitical tribe. The sons of Issachar were known for a unique contribution; they were *"men...who understood the times"* (1 Chron. 12:32).

What if the entire church of Jesus Christ were made up of wealthy individuals? Some congregations are like that. What if all in the church were destitute? Some congregations are like that too. What if they were all black, all white, all American, or all anything? You can certainly build exclusive churches if that's what you're determined to do. But if you take away the roadblocks and hang-ups of inclusion and let the Holy Spirit do what He wants to do, the church will look like the kingdom of God. Every kind of person you can imagine will be in our churches, each one bringing both the spiritual and natural gifts that have been developed by the Holy Spirit through his or her own unique experiences.[4]

3. Kingdom Diversity is Unified in Jesus Christ.

The inclusive character of the kingdom should not be interpreted to mean that anyone is to be included without first acknowledging Jesus as Savior and Lord. That is the common denominator of kingdom diversity. Even the goal of reconciliation cannot be exalted above faith in Christ. Neither is the centrality of Scripture to be questioned or compromised in exchange for racial and cultural harmony. Racial reconciliation and the Christian faith are not antithetical to one another. Both must function concurrently and should be lived out together in a juxtaposed relationship.

To remain true to Scripture, we have to carefully discern every new teaching. Because a position is supported with a few Bible verses doesn't mean that the doctrine as a whole is consistent with the purpose of God as revealed in Scripture. Individual verses must be interpreted and applied in a way that is consistent with the entirety of Scripture.

In October 1995, the Nation of Islam leader, Minister Louis Farrakhan, organized the Million Man March. The event attracted hundreds of thousands of African-American men to Capitol Hill in Washington, D.C. The goal of the gathering was for black men to demonstrate solidarity and make atonement for their sins. Notwithstanding the nature of Louis Farrakhan's beliefs and his public denunciation of Jews, whites and others, a significant number of African-American

34

Christians participated in this quasi-political demonstration.

According to Farrakhan, the real evil in the world is white supremacy. Because of this, he asserts, whites "took Jesus...and [made] him white, so that you could worship him."[5] Association on the part of Christians with this type of thinking reflects a great lack of discernment. Farrakhan's distorted image of the history and practice of Christianity and his racist rhetoric do more to harm race relations than they do to ease tensions.

Christian men of color should not compromise the centrality of Scripture to show public allegiance to their race. Similarly, white Christians ought not support racist ideologies and practices because their proponents are Caucasian. Eugene Rivers, a Boston-based Pentecostal minister and head of the interracial Ten Point Coalition, said, "The ascension of Farrakhan as a pivotal figure in the black community is a result of the failure of the black church to develop a coordinated program of evangelism and rehabilitation for black males."[6] Rivers' point is made even stronger by the fact that his father worked with both Elijah Muhammad and Malcolm X.

In Jesus' parable of the banquet, when the hall was filled with a great assortment of guests, the king noticed one who was not properly dressed.

> [12] *"'Friend,' he asked, 'how did you get in here without wedding clothes?' The man was speechless. [13] Then the king told the attendants, 'Tie him hand and foot, and throw him outside, into the darkness, where there will be weeping and gnashing of teeth.'"*   (Matt. 22:12–13)

In Luke's gospel, another passage implies that the kingdom of God will be a diversity of people unified under the lordship of Jesus

Christ. Here, Jesus was speaking about the narrow door that leads to the kingdom of God, saying that only a few will find it. He condemned those who practiced only external spirituality by saying:

> *27 "But he will reply, 'I don't know you or where you come from. Away from me, all you evildoers!'*

> *28 There will be weeping there, and gnashing of teeth, when you see Abraham, Isaac and Jacob and all the prophets in the kingdom of God, but you yourselves thrown out. 29 People will come from east and west and north and south, and will take their places at the feast in the kingdom of God. 30 Indeed there are those who are last who will be first, and first who will be last."* (Luke 13:27–30)

Jesus mentioned this on at least one other occasion. He said to the Roman centurion who had requested that He speak only a word in order to heal his daughter:

> *10 "I tell you the truth, I have not found anyone in Israel with such great faith. 11 I say to you that many will come from the east and the west, and will take their places at the feast with Abraham, Isaac and Jacob in the kingdom of heaven. 12 But the subjects of the kingdom will be thrown outside, into the darkness, where there will be weeping and gnashing of teeth."* (Matt. 8:10b–12)

The kingdom of God is always pictured as being populated by people drawn from the ends of the earth. Although diversity of race, language, gender, culture, and economic status is not specifically mentioned in this passage, you cannot collect people from the north, south, east, and west without creating a mixture of great diversity. The Jewish religious leaders were like an exclusive "ole boys' club" that was fully dedicated to hanging on to its tradition. Jesus' story makes very clear the point that the kingdom will not be a monoracial fraternity that only recruits those of "our own kind."

Unity in the kingdom is not based on race, culture, gender, economic status, or nationality. The "narrow way" does not mean a narrow target group based on age, economic status, or racial, and cultural distinction. Jesus walked away from the Pharisees' club in order to establish a kingdom of people representing every kind of diversity. Whenever you see unity based primarily on externals, important internal characteristics of the kingdom of God will always be missing.

4. Division in the Kingdom is Spiritual Vulnerability.

Whatever you believe about the extent of Satan's influence in our daily lives, this is sure: Satan is the father of lies; he is the one who sows discord and is the accuser of the brethren. His target is always relationships—an individual's relationship to God, a husband's relationship with his wife, relationships between brothers and sisters in the home, and relationships in the church and in society.

The places where tension exists between groups—whether racial, economic, or social—become key battlegrounds of spiritual warfare. Perhaps the reason Satan so consistently attacks relationships is that spiritual strongholds are built upon relational offenses. In an interracial church, the pastors and the leadership must always be on the alert to put out fires that can potentially spread into racially based disagreements. The challenge of attaining unity is to get people to focus on the issues behind the disharmony and to take their focus off the visible differences of race and culture.

Unity is a weapon of spiritual warfare. The value it provides to the strength of relationships in general cannot be underestimated. In Psalm 133, David said three things about unity: it is good and pleasant; it is like precious anointing oil; and, it is like the dew on Mount Hermon. These three points illustrate the benefits of unity within the context of family.

> [1]*How good and pleasant it is when brothers live together in unity!* [2]*It is like precious oil poured on the head, running down on the beard, running down on Aaron's beard, down upon the collar of his robes.* [3]*It is as if the dew of Hermon were falling on Mount Zion. For there the Lord bestows his blessing, even life forevermore.* (Ps. 133:1–3)

The setting of David's Psalm was the annual feast when Israel gathered as one great household in the city of Jerusalem. The adjectives *good* and *pleasant* describe the internal qualities of true unity. Oftentimes the church measures only external signs as indicators of unity. Cross-cultural relationships must be built from the inside out, not from the outside in. Achieving a mixed congregation is not equivalent to having an interracial church. The true inner quality of relationships must be measured regularly.

Commenting on verse 1 of Psalm 133, Charles H. Spurgeon wrote, "There are three things wherein it is very pleasant to behold the people of God joining in one. When they...are one in opinion...one in affection...[one] together in duty."[7] These qualities must be present internally in order for Christian fellowship to be effective as a weapon of unity in spiritual battle.

Unity is also compared to the precious oil used to consecrate and anoint Aaron for the priesthood. Thus, the association between unity and the anointing (or the equipping by the Holy Spirit) for kingdom duty is made clear. The church will engage in spiritual warfare more successfully because unity carries an anointing with it. The multiracial church, walking in a posture of unity, is equipped from head to toe (shepherd to sheep) to do battle. The acceptance and modeling of kingdom diversity in the local church setting enables the fellowship to achieve victories in other difficult areas as well. Overcoming the relational divisions that prejudice brings provides confidence and insight in the arena of spiritual warfare.

David further described unity as like the dew on Mount Hermon, cascading down its sides to Mount Zion. Mount Hermon's highest peak is approximately 9,100 feet above sea level, and its snowy white crown, set against the blue sky, glistens in the sunlight. According to *The New Unger's Bible Dictionary*, "[Mt. Hermon's] melting snows form the main source of the Jordan and the rivers that water the Damascus plateau....The snow on the mountain condenses the vapors during the summer so that abundant dews descend upon it while the surrounding country is parched."[8] The imagery of the abundance of dew depicts the freshness and peace unity provides. Peace is a powerful spiritual weapon. It acts as a watchman, always on the guard for potential problems and unwanted intruders. A person whose spirit is at peace has an acute sensitivity to the Holy Spirit. One whose soul is in turmoil can easily miss the subtle leading of the Holy Spirit and the careful discernment that accompanies His prompting. In the context of cross-cultural churches and personal relationships, peace of mind creates stability and trust.

How we relate to one another in the church affects spiritual warfare. Concerning prayer, Jesus said that when we are in agreement, the things we pray for will be granted and what we bind will be bound.

> [15] *"If your brother sins against you, go and show him his fault, just between the two of you. If he listens to you, you have won your brother over.* [16]*But if he will not listen, take one or two others along, so that 'every matter may be established by the testimony of two or three witnesses.'* [17]*If he refuses to listen to them, tell it to the church; and if he refuses to listen even to the church, treat him as you would a pagan or a tax collector.*

> [18]*I tell you the truth, whatever you bind on earth will be bound in heaven, and whatever you loose on earth will be loosed in heaven.*

> [19]*Again, I tell you that if two of you on earth agree about anything you ask for, it will be done for you by my Father in heaven.* [20]*For where two or three come together in my name, there am I with them."* (Matt. 18:15–20)

What Jesus said about binding, loosing, and the prayer of agreement was in the context of dealing with offenses between brothers and sisters in Christ. You cannot separate the spiritual power and influence of the church from the unity of the body.

In contrast, after casting out a demon, Jesus addressed the religious leaders about spiritual warfare.

> [25] *"Every kingdom divided against itself will be ruined, and every city or household divided against itself will not stand.*

Diversity: The Nature of the Kingdom

*[26]If Satan drives out Satan, he is divided against himself.
How then can his kingdom stand?"*   (Matt. 12:25b–26)

A divided church is a church with diminished power. Spiritual warfare is conducted not only in how we pray, but also in how we live and to what extent we give ground to Satan by our actions and attitudes.

5. Diversity in the Kingdom of God is Revealed in the Way We Fellowship.

Communion in the early church was quite different than today. The Lord's Supper was not only a remembering of the body and blood of Jesus Christ; it was a celebration of fellowship with one another. Evidence of the baptism of the Holy Spirit is the fruit of the Spirit, as well as the power of the Spirit. The evidence of the power and presence of the Holy Spirit beginning on the day of Pentecost was that people put away self-centeredness and were inseparably bound together. This Spirit-birthed unity was expressed in the breaking of bread.

*They devoted themselves to the apostles' teaching and to
the fellowship, to the breaking of bread and to prayer.*
(Acts 2:42)

*[46]Every day they continued to meet together in the temple
courts. They broke bread in their homes and ate together
with glad and sincere hearts, [47]praising God and enjoying
the favor of all the people. And the Lord added to their number daily those who were being saved.*   (Acts 2:46–47)

Jesus told the disciples to wait in Jerusalem for the outpouring of the Holy Spirit. Why were there forty days between the crucifixion and the outpouring of the Spirit? Only God knows all the reasons behind His timing. But we do know this: God poured out His Spirit on the day when men from all over the Roman Empire were in Jerusalem. The character of the kingdom is inclusion. It was the language barrier that gave such significance to the tongues of fire. Each man was hearing the believers praise God in his own language. Every racial, cultural, and language barrier became irrelevant in the presence of the Holy Spirit. A sign of being Spirit-filled is unity of fellowship. Conversely, Paul wrote to the Corinthians that divisions among them were evidence that they were not spiritual but carnal (1 Cor. 3:1–3).

Fellowship incorporates in its function the ability to laugh and cry with one another. Sharing in the full spectrum of human emotions cements relationships. One Sunday morning I announced to the church that we were going to have a time of fellowship on the following Sunday. I asked everyone to bring a covered dish. The following week, people could hardly wait for the service to be over. There was such a feeling of anticipation in the air. It was so exciting. Everyone brought his or her favorite foods. One international couple, however, misunderstood my request for a covered dish. They brought a covered dish with no food inside. We laughed and laughed. When they understood why we were laughing, they joined in the laughter as well. The proof of genuine fellowship is that people are relaxed and can freely express their feelings and emotions with the rest of the body. The ability of this couple to laugh at us and even with us showed that the ethnic barriers were torn down. Our feelings could be shared without losing our mutual respect for each other.

Diversity in the kingdom of God must include the accommodation of various cultural foods. What you like is not the only type of cuisine that should be made available in a cross-cultural setting. This may sound like an obvious point, but a person who has been isolated in his own culture for most of his life doesn't think about food as an expression of cultural diversity. At Christ Church, we had to spend time training the leaders and support team in hospitality. If fellowship time is scheduled around a meal, it won't be enjoyable if the attendees don't know that you have planned for their attendance and provided their preferred food choices.

6. *Christ-Centeredness and Diversity are Characteristics of Maturity in the Kingdom.*

In general, the marks of spiritual immaturity are selfishness and self-centeredness. As I mentioned previously, from my earliest days as a Christian I was convinced that we are to be Christ-centered and kingdom-centered, not culture-centered, race-centered, or self-centered.

Immature people, like children, are primarily concerned with their own needs and desires. There's nothing wrong with being immature if you are a child. And there's nothing wrong with being spiritually immature if you are a new believer. But as Paul wrote, *"When I was a child, I talked like a child, I thought like a child, I reasoned like a child. When I became a man, I put childish ways behind me"* (1 Cor. 13:11). God's desire for each Christian is for him or her to mature to the place where he or she is free from addiction to self. So then, one of the signs of maturity is caring for and serving others.

If serving in love is the mark of an individual's maturity in Christ, then serving in diversity is the mark of corporate maturity in the church. Paul wrote to the Ephesian Christians about what he foresaw as the Church at the full measure of her maturity. He stated that the ministries of the apostles, prophets, evangelists, pastors, and teachers were given to the church for the following reason:

> ...*¹²to prepare God's people for works of service, so that the body of Christ may be built up ¹³until we all reach unity in the faith and in the knowledge of the Son of God **and become mature, attaining to the whole measure of the fullness of Christ**.*   (Eph. 4:12–13, emphasis added)

Notice in the following verse how such a mature expression of the body of Christ functions:

> ...*the whole body, joined and held together by every supporting ligament, grows and builds itself up in love....*
> (Eph. 4:16)

One of the ways in which the Holy Spirit matures and prepares the church is by personally administrating diversity. He gives each one of us a gift. And as each of the various gifts and ministries supplies a contribution, the body grows and matures. The glorious church—holy and blameless, without spot or wrinkle (Eph. 5:27), also described as the bride of Christ who has made herself ready—is a church of diversity and variety, whose members are centered on Jesus Christ. The church is the expression of the kingdom of God on earth. It should reflect the congregation that surrounds the throne in the heavenly kingdom, which includes every tribe, tongue, people, and nation.

—— *Chapter 3* ——

THE MULTIETHNIC CHURCH

In 1998, Christ Church invested several thousand dollars in a communication system enabling us to translate our English preaching into Spanish. This was in response to both the Great Commission and the migration of Hispanics into the northern New Jersey suburban communities. Though the Hispanic population is not burgeoning in our area as much as in other parts of the country, there is a recognizable growth. If we want to become world-class Christians, who are sensitive to the realities of our changing communities, it is going to cost us in many different ways.

Ray Bakke, a seminary professor of urban theology, has analyzed the cultural transformation of the population in several U.S. megacities. Bakke described how this transformation is expected to affect the church:

> Of course, the challenge is also ecclesiastical, for every church and denomination will face the reality that while the church may keep the same basic functions (worship, evangelism, discipleship, stewardship, fellowship and service), the forms they take must adapt to the pluralized and kaleidoscopic realities of a twenty-four-hour city. Like supermarkets, hospitals and police departments, churches will require

day pastors and night pastors for twenty-four-hour environments in all languages, cultures and class groups, now residing in the same communities.[1]

The church needs to respond to the dynamics of monocultural communities growing into multicultural cities. Bakke added, "In 1900, 8 percent of the world's population lived in cities. By the year 2000, that number will be nearly 50 percent."[2]

The body of Christ must be able to thrive within a diverse society. You may not live in what is considered a megacity, but the same phenomenon is taking place at various levels everywhere. The small towns of America—towns where at one time relatively few people moved in or away—are seeing small groups of internationals becoming citizens of their communities. Who would have thought thirty years ago that Seattle, Washington, would evolve into a racially and culturally diverse metropolis? Yet today large segments of Japanese, Chinese, Hispanics, Koreans, African-Americans, and other people of color have made Seattle their home.

The question, then, for each Christian who takes the Great Commission seriously is this: *Are you prepared to be a member, a participant, or even the leader of a world-class church?* In every generation, there are churches that grow and churches that decline. Being part of a congregation that is losing members, influence, and impact is no fun. Leading one is even more painful. In most cases, the problem is not that people do not love God—and it's certainly not that God doesn't love them. It's simply that the world is changing while people remain stubbornly fixed to traditional methods, perspectives, and preferences. Consequently, their churches become irrelevant. In the twenty-first century, healthy, growing congregations will be those of which multiculturalism is a major component. This is an inescapable reality, both now and in the distant future.

A world-class, culturally inclusive church does not simply emerge because the neighborhood becomes more diverse. Earlier I cited my research project involving two churches in Corona, Queens, which illustrated this very point. The church is not always on track with the community with regard to its vision for growth and diversity.

A MODEL OF THE WORLD-CLASS CHURCH

Becoming globally minded is an ethical issue and not one of preference or trend. I began several years ago preparing my congregation for the coming sociological changes by preaching a series of messages entitled *Becoming a World-Changer*. It has been my observation that there are certain distinctions that make a church a world-class church and a Christian a world-changer. These characteristics are exemplified in Acts chapter 11.

1. World-Class Churches Are Congregations That Thrive in a Changing Community.

The Antioch Christians practiced their faith by building a world-class church, harvesting souls of different racial and cultural backgrounds. The church at Antioch, more than any other church in the New Testament, was responsible for building a bridge to transport the gospel across the great cultural and ethnic divides of the first century. Several key characteristics of the congregation at Antioch set it apart as a world-class church.

> [19]*Now those who had been scattered by the persecution in connection with Stephen traveled as far as Phoenicia, Cyprus and Antioch, telling the message only to Jews.* [20]*Some of them, however, men from Cyprus and Cyrene, went to*

Antioch and began to speak to Greeks also, telling them the good news about the Lord Jesus. [21]The Lord's hand was with them, and a great number of people believed and turned to the Lord.

[22]News of this reached the ears of the church at Jerusalem, and they sent Barnabas to Antioch. [23]When he arrived and saw the evidence of the grace of God, he was glad and encouraged them all to remain true to the Lord with all their hearts. [24]He was a good man, full of the Holy Spirit and faith, and a great number of people were brought to the Lord. (Acts 11:19–24)

In the first century, persecution arose in Jerusalem. This caused many Christians to migrate as far as three hundred miles northwest of Jerusalem, to the city of Antioch. Fear of annihilation did not stop these Christians from sharing their faith, however. As they were running for their lives, they were sharing the good news of Jesus Christ. Persecution and uncertainty of life fueled the gospel. Sociological pressure resulted in increased evangelism. For this reason, Tertullian, one of the first-century church fathers, wrote, "The blood of Christians is seed. The more we are mowed down the more we grow." This simple but powerful observation is still true today. The church of the Lord Jesus thrives in an environment of resistance and pluralism.

According to Michael Green, a noted scholar on the subject of evangelism:

[Antioch on the Orontes was] the capital of the province of Syria, governed by a proconsul in charge of two legions. It was the third city in the Empire, with its own Games, a

48

tremendous building program financed jointly by Augustus and Herod, a large and influential but very lax Jewish population, and a reputation for immorality of which even Juvenal disapproved. It was the centre for diplomatic relations with the vassal states of the East, and was, in fact, a meeting point for many nationalities, a place where barriers between Jew and Gentile were very slight.

As one of the largest cities in the Empire, and one of the great commercial centres of antiquity, with business connections all over the world, Antioch saw the coming and going of all sorts of people from every quarter of the globe.[3]

The uniqueness of the city from a global perspective was that the gospel had not yet been preached there on any large scale. Because of Antioch's geographical location and economic influence on the region, how the people of the city responded to the gospel and the manifestations of God's presence could easily influence the world.

Seleucus I had founded the city in approximately 300 B.C. and named it after his father, Antiochus. In the New Testament era, the influx of Jewish believers into the city precipitated certain changes. Keep in mind that change does not take place, nor is it welcomed, unless there is a need in the hearts of the people who stand to benefit from that change. Apparently the citizens of Antioch were unsatisfied with their empty pluralistic philosophies, cult religions, and worldly tolerance.

The idea of various cultures, ethnic groups, and races dwelling together in an influential city is not uncommon. This has been the practice ever since the building of the Tower of Babel in the city of Shinar (Gen. 11:1–9). First-century Antioch was considered a world-class city. In fact, many modern scholars and historians refer to it as "the Paris of the Ancient World" because of its cultural splendor, beautiful architecture (including the temple of Artemis), amphitheater, and royal palaces.[4] Nevertheless, the common worship of the goddess Artemis left the citizens of this port city spiritually restless and empty. The introduction of Christianity was an answer to the spiritual vacuum of the people of Antioch.

Not only was the change in spiritual climate a needed one, but the community was also changing in regards to its agricultural, economic, and trade practices, as well as in its interest in philosophical reasoning. During this period in Antioch's history, Green comments, "An interesting factor is the increase in abstract philosophical terms like Power, Renewal, Creation, Pleasure, Life, Salvation, and Enjoyment. [This] shows that when Christians spoke of joy, salvation, power, and eternal life, their words would be understood, and the contemporary climate was one which was very interested in such concepts."[5] The gospel came at a very opportune time.

The term "Christian" was first used at Antioch because of the broad impact of the message of Christ upon the community (Acts 11:26). Many people were turning to Christ. Within the Roman Empire, the church at Antioch played a larger role in the early stages of Christianity than did any other church except for the church at Jerusalem. Situated on one of the most important trade routes of the day, Antioch's geographical location helped position the church to change the world. Thus, this racially diverse congregation became a world-class church by flowing with the tide of its changing community.

Similarly, many communities in the United States are changing. Racial, cultural, economical, and housing changes are all occurring right before our eyes. Rather than fleeing to more comfortable, predictable environments, the world-class church stays and becomes part of the change. These types of churches are interested in using the growth of their cities as launching pads for ministry. They run toward densely populated communities rather than fleeing. Innovative methods of ministry are developed in an attempt to serve the new ethnic groups moving into their neighborhoods. The world-class church sees changing communities as new mission fields where the gospel of Jesus Christ must be proclaimed.

2. World-Class Churches Have World-Class Leaders.

The Jerusalem apostles were very wise to send Barnabas to Antioch during the outbreak of revival. The cross-cultural city of Antioch needed a cross-cultural leader, and ultimately, a cross-cultural leadership team. Multicultural inclinations and experience were not the only prerequisites for the apostolic mission team. The leader also had to be sensitive, tactful, and diplomatic. A cross-cultural ambassador was what this assignment required.

Barnabas was a Levite born in Cyprus (Acts 4:36). Cyprus was a bicultural city, and a Levite was trained to be sensitive in his service to God's people. In fact, the name *Barnabas* means "son of encouragement or consolation." It's interesting to note that the apostles called him Barnabas rather than using his birth name, Joseph.

F. F. Bruce, in his analysis of Acts, states that the word "son" in the meaning of the name *Barnabas* was a familiar Semitic idiom which indicated a man's character.[6] The name further signifies the tender and sensitive side of Barnabas' personality, which was obviously apparent to all who knew him. Thus, Barnabas was an encourager. He was the man for the job in the culturally diverse city of Antioch.

Cyprus is an island situated near the northeast section of the Mediterranean Sea. It passed from Egyptian hands into Roman possession circa 22 B.C. Its close proximity to Syria made it easy for Jews to settle there from Palestine.[7] The city was inhabited by Jews, Greeks, Romans, and people of other Hellenic cultures. Cyprus prided itself on its tolerance of diversity and pluralism. Living in such a culturally diverse city required a working knowledge of the languages of trade and the marketplace. Thus, Barnabas knew how to navigate his way through the kaleidoscope of cultural diversity.

During the time in which Barnabas would have come to Christ, many priests and Levites were becoming obedient to the faith (Acts 6:7). The role of a Levite was to carry out the duties of temple service, thereby assisting the priests in the ministry of presenting the needs of the people to God. The job required faithfulness and a desire to live honestly before God. Once Barnabas became obedient to the Christian faith, he began to grow as an authentic reconciler. When the message of the good news of God's love for mankind spread to the cross-cultural city of Antioch, Barnabas was able to fit right in with what God was doing. The divine purpose for his religious background, education, and bicultural upbringing became clear and meaningful.

For this unique ministry opportunity, a cross-cultural team, representing the diversity of the community, was needed. And such was the case with the ministry team at this model church. Shortly after his arrival in Antioch to pastor the new congregation, Barnabas apparently realized that his leadership was lacking in some areas. He sent to Tarsus for Paul to come and provide the primary leadership for this growing work (Acts 11:25–26).

Tarsus was also a bicultural city, a trading center famous to many cultures because of its access to the Mediterranean Sea. Therefore, Paul, a product of that city, was a bicultural man.

A common misconception is that Paul's name changed from *Saul* to *Paul* after his Christian conversion. This was not the case. The use of both names was an attempt to relate to two different cultures. Paul used his original Jewish name, Saul, whenever he was interacting in a strictly Jewish setting. His Roman name, Paul, was used more frequently because of his primary calling to share the gospel with Gentiles. Consequently, it's easy to see why God involved Paul in the culturally diverse congregation at Antioch. He and Barnabas labored together as a dynamic team to build a world-class church.

Years later, as recorded in Acts 13, the cross-cultural team of elders, formed around the foundational ministry gifts of Paul and Barnabas, was still functioning. Luke wrote, *"In the church at Antioch there were prophets and teachers: Barnabas, Simeon called Niger, Lucius of Cyrene, Manaen (who had been brought up with Herod the tetrarch) and Saul"* (Acts 13:1). Thom Hopler, in his book *A World of Difference*, has these insights about this leadership team:

> Notice also that Barnabas and Paul are not listed together. They are not at the top of the heap, lording it over the other three. They are not at the bottom, as if to say in false humility that they do not have any influence. They are coequal leaders, and so Luke splits them, I think, purposely to show this.[8]

The eldership is also a cultural, ethnic, and socioeconomic representation of the community and the church. This unique team of elders, expressing strength in diversity, was like a "dream team" in an athletic contest. They were able to present a relevant perspective of the Scriptures and the heart of God to their multiethnic community.

The three other elders also brought a significant strength of ministry and unique diversity to the team. Simeon, Lucius, and Manaen were remarkable prophets and teachers. They were the ones who had heard from the Holy Spirit about the need to set apart Paul and Barnabas for their apostolic call (Acts 13:2). These men were not token representatives, chosen mainly because of their ethnic backgrounds. They had legitimate, *bona fide* ministry gifts that were on a par with those of Paul and Barnabas. This qualified them to serve as elders of this great church.

Simeon, called Niger, was an African. *Niger* means, literally, "the black." Lucius was a common name in the first-century Greco-Roman world. Lucius was a Greek. Manaen is a Greek form of the Hebrew word *menahem*, meaning "comforter." Manaen was a Jew. The Scripture attaches the phrase "who had been brought up with Herod the tetrarch" to Manaen's name. This description reflects the ancient title of "foster brother," and according to F. F. Bruce, "[this title] was given to boys of the same age as royal princes, who were taken to court to be brought up with them."[9] Manaen was the childhood playmate of Herod Antipas (the younger son of Herod the Great), who was tetrarch from 4 B.C. to A.D. 39 and ruled Galilee and Perea. Manaen brought not only ethnic diversity to the team of elders, but also the component of socio-economic variety. Having been the childhood playmate of a king's son exposed Manaen to the highest level of social conduct and etiquette to be found in the ancient world.

Verse 1 of Acts 13 introduces these elders in two ways: first, by their ministry gifts, and second, by their ethnic backgrounds. This introduction of the leaders establishes the reality that ethnic diversity was fully represented among the church's leadership and was considered an important feature. The Antioch church had a functioning model of diversity.

If the church of the twenty-first century is going to be multicultural, the price must be paid to develop leadership teams after the Antioch model. Where there is potential for division, people like Barnabas (a bicultural exhorter) must be sought out and supported by similarly gifted people. But often the power structures of multiracial churches are monoracial. This is not a biblical model, nor is it a proper social model.

The incident in Acts 6 with the Hebrew and Hellenistic widows squabbling over injustice must be duly noted as a potential problem every time different cultures function together. Equality and proper representation must be visibly demonstrated. The congregation must be able to look on the platform and see people who look like themselves. I am not suggesting tokenism, the appointment of "yes men," or the installation of unqualified leaders. Leaders must be sought out as Barnabas sought out Paul. Leaders must be trained, mentored, and developed so that the people-groups in the congregation are represented, over a period of time, in the leadership structure. This must be the commitment of any church that wants to become world-class.

3. A World-Class Church is Composed of World-Class Christians.

A leader's effectiveness always depends on the willingness of his or her followers to be cooperative. Robert Kelley writes in *The Power of Followership*, "When I pointed out that some actually gave up leadership roles because they preferred the work and rewards of following, they wondered if these people were not simply 'happy losers' who realized they couldn't make the leadership grade and had resigned themselves to their predicament."[10] Often we applaud leaders for their great accomplishments and never mention the role of the followers who served quietly behind the scenes. Where would the ministry of Paul have been without those protégés who labored to help him fulfill his mission? What Bible would we have to read today had not the apostles had capable deacons to serve them? I am not making light of the sovereignty and omnipotence of God. He does not need any of us. I am simply pointing out that the supporting cast cannot be ignored, even in the presence of great, world-class leaders.

The congregants in any local church play an invaluable role. If there are no people, a church cannot exist. Although the Scriptures don't teach a congregational or democratic form of government, the Bible instructs elders not to lord their leadership over the flock (1 Pet. 5:3). The sensitivity of pastors in overseeing and equipping their congregations helps the members develop into significant contributors.

Nothing will be accomplished if the congregation doesn't voluntarily buy into the corporate vision. In a multiracial church, kingdom diversity and multiculturalism must be clearly and repeatedly articulated so that everyone understands the dynamics of the vision.

The Antioch model shows that the church had a vision to accept ethnic diversity in every stratum of its infrastructure. The diversity of its elders shows that the church's leaders were sensitive to the various cultures present in the congregation. The members of the congregation must have known that they were respected, loved, and honored by the leadership. If people feel that they are invisible, they will not buy into the leader's vision, and ultimately they will go where they will be heard and celebrated.

The formation of a world-class congregation begins as diverse people find themselves relaxing in the presence of the group. They sense a freedom to worship God according to their cultural mores. A spirit of accommodation prevails because of the foundation of trust laid by the elders. Creating an environment where people's personal needs are met fosters their willingness to serve the vision of the house.

The elders at Christ Church are committed to understanding the feelings of people at the grass roots level. The larger the church becomes, the more we find ourselves struggling to understand the perspectives of people who are new to the church and to a diverse congregation. In an attempt to understand the congregation's concerns, we poll the congregation every two years to get their opinions on guest speakers, sermon topics, worship styles, race relations, and reconciliation issues. We have found that this allows people to anonymously voice legitimate concerns.

In a church that espouses and models racial reconciliation, the pastors must understand that their people are giving up certain things that the broader society, and even the greater body of Christ, are not willing to relinquish. They may subordinate their preferences for a certain type of preaching style, worship format, or communication style to accommodate the inclusive models required in a multicultural setting.

Many of my congregants had to readjust their relationships with family and friends (even other Christians) who couldn't accept or appreciate a cross-cultural life or ministry. This concession may even extend to family members who despise the fact that a sibling or parent worships at a multiracial church. Ridicule and rejection from the people you love is always difficult. Thus, world-class Christians want their leaders to know and appreciate the sacrifices they have made to sit under their leadership.

4. World-Class Churches See Problems As Opportunities in Disguise.

Some time ago, an American shoe manufacturing company sent two salesmen to the Australian outback to drum up new business. After several weeks, the first salesman wired back to the States, "Shoe business here is lousy; the natives don't wear shoes." Two days later the second salesman wired back, "Shoe business here is great; the natives don't wear shoes." Interestingly enough, both salesmen saw people with the same custom of walking barefoot. One saw the lack of shoes as a problem, while the other saw an opportunity.

World-class churches have been able to take their problems and turn them into divine opportunities. Such was the case in Antioch. The church was started because persecuted Christians ran for their lives from Jerusalem to Antioch. As they were fleeing, they continued to fulfill the Great Commission—that is, to make disciples of all nations. These Christians, along with the converts they made, were the very ones who became the founding members of the Antioch church. They took a problem (persecution) and turned it into an opportunity (disciple making). Our English word *opportunity* comes from the Latin and means "toward the port." It suggests a ship taking advantage of the wind and tide to arrive safely in the harbor.[11]

World-class churches are opportunity makers. There is an interesting Chinese word for "crisis." Earle H. Ballou points out that this word "is made up of two characters that, when pronounced sound like 'way gee.' Each of these is half a word, the first being *danger* and the second *opportunity*. Hence, a crisis is literally a 'dangerous opportunity.'"[12]

Opportunities never make the grand announcement, "I'm an opportunity; take advantage of me!" Rather, the opportunity is masked in the form of a crisis or problem. Most people do not see the potential miracle because it often looks like a mess at the onset. Barnabas could easily have taken the attitude that a bunch of cowards had defected from the church to avoid being confronted for their faith and thought, *I'm going to baby-sit them with some words of encouragement.* Had he not discerned the real nature of the problem and formulated a positive attitude toward the fledgling group, a world-class church would not have been birthed.

Wrong attitudes blind us from seeing opportunities. In the infancy of our church, I used to complain religiously to my wife that I did not have the leaders I needed to accomplish what the Lord had called me to do. When she would no longer listen to my complaining, I would complain to myself. One day Marlinda told me to just stop complaining and do something about the problem. "If you don't have the leaders you need," she said, "turn this problem into an opportunity. Let God make *you* a greater leader."

After my frustration subsided, I thought to myself, *Hey, her statement makes a whole lot of sense.* I immediately began putting together a variety of leadership development programs. In an attempt to develop what the church needed, we taught everything from mentoring to theology and even created personalized reading programs. Today, we have strong leaders on many different tiers of church life. I'm also frequently called upon to conduct leadership seminars across the country and in other nations. These opportunities evolved because I turned a problem into an opportunity. What is causing you the biggest headache? Turn it into an opportunity!

I came across a witty little poem that emphasizes this very point. Let me share it with you.

The Oyster

There once was an oyster whose story I tell,
Who found that sand had got under his shell;
Just one little grain, but it gave him much pain.
For oysters have feelings although they're so plain.
Now did he berate the working of Fate,
Which had led him to such a deplorable state?
Did he curse out the government, call for an election?
No; as he lay on the shelf, he said to himself:
"If I cannot remove it, I'll try to improve it."

So the years rolled by as the years always do,
And he came to his ultimate destiny—stew.
And this small grain of sand which had bothered him so,
Was a beautiful pearl, all richly aglow.
Now this tale has a moral—for isn't it grand
What an oyster can do with a morsel of sand:
What couldn't we do if we'd only begin
With all of the things that get under our skin.[13]

5. *World-Class Churches Are Missions Minded.*

The Antioch church began as a mission, albeit an unintended one, and evolved into a megachurch that supported strategically planned missions. The first mention of the Antioch church investing in missions occurred shortly after its inception:

> [27]*During this time some prophets came down from Jerusalem to Antioch. One of them, named Agabus, stood up and through the Spirit predicted that a severe famine would spread over the entire Roman world. (This happened during the reign of Claudius.) The disciples, each according to his ability, decided to provide help for the brothers living in Judea. This they did, sending their gift to the elders by Barnabas and Saul.* (Acts 11:27–30)

Following Agabus' prophecy of a forthcoming famine and its obvious impact on Judea, the Christians at Antioch felt the burden to support their brothers. Their desire to provide financial assistance was neither an edict nor a suggestion given by Paul and Barnabas to the church. The entire body felt the spontaneous urge to respond generously to the prophetic word by helping in a practical way. The potential of widespread social problems such as starvation and sickness, along with economic failure and criminal wrongdoing, was apparent.

From a spiritual perspective, the problem of famine could easily have hindered the spread of the gospel. William Booth, founder of the Salvation Army, said, "A man cannot hear you when his stomach is empty. Feed him, and he will listen." How true!

By sending funds to aid the Judean Christians, Antioch exhibited its concern for the entire body of Christ. Investing in missions is an investment in the global harvesting of souls. People will be brought to Christ in other parts of the world as a result of prayerful financial investments in missions. The world-class church sees evangelism and social reformation as two important missions of the church. The Antioch church saw investing in the Judean Christians as a social responsibility.

Acts 13 provides us with another example of the Antioch church's commitment to missions. They were willing to give up Paul and Barnabas, their primary leaders, in order to see them fulfill their apostolic ministries and thereby serve the larger body of Christ. The missionary journeys of Paul and Barnabas resulted in scores of churches being planted and thousands of people coming to Christ. These daughter churches would also develop and train people for world missions (Phil. 4:15).

Apparently, the Antioch Christians wanted to be kept abreast of the workings of the Holy Spirit around the world. Paul and Barnabas stayed in contact with the church in Antioch. It served as their home base. Upon their return, the two apostles would report all that was happening in the new churches. The Antioch church was not detached from the joy of missions, the needs of the churches, or the responsibility to provide ongoing care for the missionaries (Acts 14:26–28).

Investing in missions is also a sign that a church shares in the virtue of generosity. Generosity is an important aspect of the nature of God. It was God's generosity that caused Him to send His Son to make atonement for us. Scripture states, *"A generous man will prosper; he who refreshes others will himself be refreshed"* (Prov. 11:25). When we refresh others in their times of need, we will be refreshed in our time of need. The law of sowing and reaping (Gal. 6:7) goes into effect, and the missions-minded church prospers accordingly.

6. *World-Class Churches Release People in Their Gifts.*

The world-class church understands the uniqueness of its assignment to reach the lost and the need for each member to be a participant in this worthy endeavor. Barnabas made the decision to send to Tarsus for Paul because the ideas of *potential*, *purpose*, and *plan* were in his heart for the Antioch church. The church's potential could not have been reached unless Barnabas received the adequate help this particular congregation needed. All the right ingredients were present, even though they existed in an undeveloped state. This church had great potential, yet it could not be unlocked until the right gifts were operating regularly in its midst.

We too must reach our potential in order to fulfill our purpose. No one starts out with the goal of influencing people on a global level. This goal often is born after success on a local or regional level has been achieved. Barnabas realized God's purpose for the church, yet without the right gifts, the purpose would not have been accomplished.

A church that is clear about its mission attracts the gifts needed to fulfill its purpose. The presence of a clear purpose sends a loud signal, declaring, "There's a place for you to fit in here. You won't sit idly by and watch. We know how to develop and use your gift. Join our team." This kind of church intentionally begins the process of molding and shaping the gifts in its midst. One cannot have a world-class church composed of world-class people and not know what to do with their spiritual gifts. In such a nonproductive environment, people leave the church out of frustration, with the aim of finding greener pastures elsewhere.

There is a temptation to take an overly spiritualized approach to gift recognition. The simplest approach is sometimes the best—that is, to discover what a person enjoys doing. That sense of joy and satisfaction may be an indication of God's gifts and calling. The movie *Chariots of Fire* features a missionary family by the name of Liddell. In a transitional moment in the film, Eric Liddell, an athlete, is trying to discover his life's purpose. His missionary sister confronts him about how his running is keeping him from his missions work. She asks, "Why do you run so much and spend so little time in God's work on the mission field?"

Eric replies, "God made me fast, and when I run I can sense His pleasure."

This is how people in a world-class church should feel: *God gave me a gift, and when I use it, I can sense His pleasure.*

Seeing and knowing what to do with someone's gift requires wisdom from God. Gifts must be paired with the needs of the church and community. Some gifts are for use in the local church, while others must serve the needs of the neighborhood. For example, I have a friend who pastors a church in Wilkensburg, an urban area within the Pittsburgh city limits. The town gave him a dilapidated school building that seemed useless and beyond repair. One of the members of the congregation applied for and received several grants totaling several million dollars. Now the building is used to house many of the church's social programs. Another member came up with the idea of allocating space in the newly renovated building so that the congregation could partner with several nonprofit groups to further serve the practical needs of the community.

My prayer is that God would open our eyes to see the many types of gifts He has set within the church. These gifts have been created to meet the needs within and without the church's walls. When we recognize and activate the gifts within our midst, the church will begin to reach its full potential and be well on the way to accomplishing its purpose.

Chapter 4

GOD'S PERSPECTIVE ON RACE

Several months ago an article appeared in a local newspaper about how traditional racial categories are changing. One woman featured in the story had a father who was part Korean and part Mexican. Her mother was the child of a white and a black relationship. As the product of such a multiethnic background, she struggled to determine which race she identified with most.

Race is not a big issue for children of multiracial or multiethnic families. It is only when they discover how important race is to everyone else that they begin to feel self-conscious. Most people are monoracial and never have to deal with such a deep, personal identity crisis. In a world where so much is made of race, to belong to no particular race became, for this woman, a lifelong struggle.

Uniqueness, diversity, and the individual expression of an underlying unity is God's purpose for the church, the family, and the world. This type of relationship between the parts that make up the whole is essentially good because it's what God Himself is like. The Trinity is the perfect expression of unity with diversity.

Today, what is often called diversity is really individualism gone to a bizarre extreme. We live in a fragmented society where the schisms, cliques, and divisions are widening every day. Consequently, racially based tensions in every major city have grown to the point that they periodically overflow into some kind of physical conflict. The church has not been exempt from this kind of tension. Unfortunately, the church of today looks far too much like the unredeemed world.

In our divided communities, blacks worship with blacks, Hispanics with Hispanics, whites with whites, and Native Americans with Native Americans. This division exists even though each group calls Jesus Christ the Lord and Savior of the world and acknowledges kinship with one another in Christ. Many political and social leaders acknowledge that racial fragmentation is one of the greatest problems America faces and that this trend will continue in the future.

As always, the challenge for the church is to be a light to the world. Can the church become a model of what the kingdom of God is supposed to be—righteousness, peace, and joy in the Holy Ghost? A great tragedy will occur if the church becomes increasingly unresponsive to one of the greatest needs of society.

THE ORIGIN OF DIVERSITY

As Christians, we all agree that God is the creator of the universe and of mankind. But we must also consider the fact that He created every one of us completely unique and strikingly different from all others. When the apostle Paul addressed the philosophers in the Areopagus on Mars Hill in Athens, his purpose was to construct a line of reasoning that would lead them to faith in Jesus Christ. In his discussion, he made reference to the sovereignty of God in cultural distinctions:

> [24] *"The God who made the world and everything in it is the Lord of heaven and earth and does not live in temples built by hands. And he is not served by human hands, as if he*

needed anything, because he himself gives all men life and breath and everything else. From one man he made every nation of men, that they should inhabit the whole earth; and he determined the times set for them and the exact places where they should live. God did this so that men would seek him and perhaps reach out for him and find him, though he is not far from each one of us." (Acts 17:24–27)

Notice what was said about the origin of diversity: *"From one man he made every nation of men."* Every people-group came from a single source, Adam. The first created humans were given the commission to multiply and fill the earth. This was the mandate that caused all the future variations in mankind to come.

The farther in history we are removed from creation, the more diversity exists among the descendants of Adam and Eve. It's important to note that this increasing diversity is not an accident that occurred over time. The Scripture says that God has *"determined the times set for them and the exact places where they should live"* (Acts 17:26).

The express intent of God to create diversity was demonstrated very early in the history of mankind. After the great flood, all the nations of the world descended from Noah through his three sons, Shem, Ham, and Japheth. There is an interesting comment in Scripture about the sixth generation of Noah's descendants: *"And two sons were born to Eber; the name of the one was Peleg* [literally meaning *division*], *for in his days the earth was divided"* (Gen. 10:25). The genealogy of Noah concludes with these words:

[1] *These are the clans of Noah's sons, according to their lines of descent, within their nations. From these the nations spread out over the earth after the flood. Now the whole*

*world had one language and a common speech....⁴Then they
said, "Come, let us build ourselves a city, with a tower that
reaches to the heavens, so that we may make a name for
ourselves and not be scattered over the face of the whole
earth."* (Genesis 10:32–11:1, 4)

The Tower of Babel was man's attempt to stop the dispersion of nations. Obviously, the scattering of the nations would increase the diversity of language, culture, and in time, physical appearance. Two other things are evident: 1) that men were unified in their determination to prevent diversity and to maintain cultural and ethnic uniformity; and, 2) that God was equally determined that diversity develop. Such a battle of wills is, of course, no contest.

There are many things that happen in this world that do not serve the plan and purpose of God, but which are allowed to continue, at least for a time. The dispersion of people was such an essential part of God's plan that it required an extraordinary intervention. God "came down," confused their language, and forced those building the tower and the city to be scattered all over the face of the earth. Can you imagine a world with one kind of human, one kind of plant, one kind of animal, and one kind of food to eat? How boring! The wonder of God's expanding creation is how all the expressions of diversity compliment each other. Diversity among nationalities, races, cultures, and ethnic groups was an indispensable ingredient in the plan of God regarding mankind.

A final note from Paul's address on Mars Hill has to do with the unifying "glue" that holds together all of this diversity. Scripture declares God's sovereign will for mankind: *"that they should seek God, if perhaps they might grope for Him and find Him, though He is not far from each one of us"* (Acts 17:27 NAS). His divine purpose is that all

racial and ethnic groups find their unity and purpose in their relationship with Him, their common creator.

God has ordained that the human race exist as a *university*, which
means literally, "diversity with unity." This was the premeditated plan
in the heart of a loving God before the dawn of time. And God should
rightfully take sole credit for the idea of diversity. After the process
was set in motion at creation, *"God saw all that he had made, and it
was very good"* (Gen. 1:31).

UNCOMFORTABLE WITH DIVERSITY

I recently read an article about a woman in Louisiana who, in the
process of applying for a marriage license, discovered that she was an
octoroon (a person of one-eighth Negro ancestry). She had all the features of a white person, including blue eyes and brunette hair. She had
been married several times before, and all her husbands thought she
was white. But a closer look at her birth certificate revealed that her
grandmother was black. The woman and her fiancé were shocked and
distraught over her discovery.

While God clearly loves diversity, much of His creation has a
problem with it. Too often Christians develop their ideas about God
from their own perceptions rather than from the Bible. In other words,
they create a God after their own image. Some people go to great lengths
to justify their prejudice and racism by attributing these same attributes
to God. They misuse the Scriptures to support the notion that God hates
the diversity He has created, and that He is actually a racist Himself.

Common sense should tell us that when we start with a premise
contrary to the nature of God, the philosophical, theological, and political dogmas that result can be terribly destructive. Consider the Na-
zism of Hitler and the Communism of Marx and Lenin. Any theology

that is skewed by fear or an aversion to diversity can have a devastating effect on people. Those who spew these divisive attitudes hate others simply because of their diversity and justify their hatred by calling it the will of God. The targets of this perverted thinking wind up hating themselves instead of rejoicing that they are created in God's image.

A fuller discussion of accepting and enjoying the person God made you to be is contained in chapter 9. The point that must be made here is this: While many use race to build walls between people, a sincere study of Scripture reveals that racial diversity is another example of the greatness of God's wisdom and creativity.

A Spiritual Definition of Race

Jesus taught us to pray for the kingdom this way: "Thy kingdom come. Thy will be done, On earth as it is in heaven" (Matt. 6:10 NAS). One of the prerequisites to extending the influence of God's kingdom on earth is to see things as He sees them, including the characteristics and qualities of the kingdom. We have to renew our minds and our thinking in a way that is sometimes contrary to the wisdom of the world. God's perspective on racial differences, which is fundamentally different from ours, is an ongoing theme throughout the Bible, particularly the New Testament. It often takes more than a few Scriptures to renew our thinking, but here are several principles and verses to get us started.

1. From God's Perspective There Are Only Two People-Groups on the Earth—Two Families That Descended from Two Men.

So it is written: "The first man Adam became a living being"; the last Adam, a life-giving spirit. (1 Cor. 15:45)

God sees each of us either as a member of the family lineage of Adam, who fell into sin, or in the family of Christ, whose righteousness is imputed to all those related to Him. We are in Adam by birth, and in Christ by faith. God's perspective is always one of distinguishing between the obedient and disobedient.

2. God Traces Our Ancestry in Spiritual Terms, Not by Blood Relationships.

Understand, then, that those who believe are children of Abraham. (Gal. 3:7)

[39]*"Abraham is our father," [the Pharisees] answered. "If you were Abraham's children," said Jesus, "then you would do the things Abraham did....*[44]*You belong to your father, the devil, and you want to carry out your father's desire."*

(John 8:39, 44)

The Jews, particularly the Pharisees, went to great lengths to establish and verify their ethnic heritage because in their minds, God's concern and preference were only for the descendants of Abraham. Jesus reaffirmed that the Father categorizes people by their spiritual connection and not by natural pedigree. The Jews were greatly prejudiced against the children of Hagar and thought of themselves as superior. To this day, a conflict exists between Israel and Palestine.

In his letter to the Galatians, Paul took an old, pharisaic allegory and turned it around (Gal. 4:21–31). Paul suggested that the Jews who rejected Christ were in fact the children of the bondwoman (Hagar, the natural mother of Ishmael and all modern-day Arabs). Gentile believers in Christ were said to be the children of the free woman (Sarah, the natural mother of Isaac and all modern-day Jews). You can see why the leaders of the synagogue reacted so violently to Paul's preaching.

3. In God's Eyes, All Christians Are of the Same Race.

> *[9]But you are a chosen race, a royal priesthood, a holy nation, a people for God's own possession, that you may proclaim the excellencies of Him who has called you out of darkness into His marvelous light; [10]for you once were not a people, but now you are the people of God.*
>
> (1 Pet. 2:9–10 NAS)

Scripture makes it clear that God has one family. He is the Father of all His children. Thus, all His children fall into one race: people made pure by the atoning death of Jesus Christ.

4. In Christ, All Physical, Social, and Economic Characteristics by Which Believers Can Be Categorized Are Done Away With.

> [28]There is neither Jew nor Greek, there is neither slave nor free man, there is neither male nor female; for you are all one in Christ Jesus. [29]And if you belong to Christ, then you are Abraham's offspring, heirs according to promise.   (Gal 3:28–29 NAS)

> *...a renewal in which there is no distinction between Greek and Jew, circumcised and uncircumcised, barbarian, Scythian, slave and freeman, but Christ is all, and in all.*
>
> (Col. 3:11 NAS)

> *[13]For by one Spirit we were all baptized into one body, whether Jews or Greeks, whether slaves or free, and we were*

all made to drink of one Spirit. *¹⁴For the body is not one
member, but many.*   (1 Cor. 12:13–14 NAS)

The triune God, who exists as Father, Son, and Holy Spirit, is one
in image, likeness, and nature (Gen. 1:26). Consequently, Moses de-
clared to the Israelites, *"Hear, O Israel: The Lord our God, the Lord is
one"* (Deut. 6:4). The Hebrew word used here for "one" is *echad*, which
signifies unity.

God exists as a multiplicity with unity. Is it surprising then, that
in creating man in His image, God's plan would be for mankind to exist
as a multiplicity with unity? In the kingdom of God, there is one race of
redeemed men and women, expressing the inexhaustible variety and
creativity of our Lord. The diversity of creation is brought into perfect
unity by Christ and the kingdom of God.

A radical change will take place in our thinking when we begin to
view all believers as God does. If we are, as Scripture clearly teaches,
one race, then the walls of separation among Christians must come
down. One illustration I use to depict unity of race is Paul's pronounce-
ment of unity regarding married couples (Eph. 5:28–31). The covenant of marriage results in the husband and wife being viewed as one;
no longer are they two separate entities. Similarly, the covenant of
salvation joins every believer to Christ and to others as members of the
family of God.

God dwells in the heart of every believer. As Paul stated at Mars
Hill, *"The God who made the world and all things in it, since He is Lord
of heaven and earth, does not dwell in temples made with hands"* (Acts
17:24 NAS). As a Christian, I cannot love God and at the same time hate
the people in whom He lives. I cannot love His church and declare a
preference against the living stones that make up the spiritual house.

True conversion is evident when a person repents and allows the Spirit of God to come in and transform him, thus making him a new creation. A convert to the kingdom of God should act as an ambassador of that kingdom. His desire should be to model the perceptions and behavior of the One he represents. Since he has been made new by the indwelling presence of the Holy Spirit, hatred of other people, or even prejudice against or preference for them, cannot abide in his heart without grieving and quenching the Spirit of God.

RACIAL RANKINGS

The fullest expression of God's nature and purpose was revealed in the person of Jesus Christ and the new covenant He inaugurated. The Jews had a fundamental misunderstanding of God and His purpose. God had chosen Israel as His covenant people to be the keepers of the Law and the nation from whom the Messiah would come. But the purpose of God from the beginning was that in Abraham's seed (that is, in Christ), the entire world would be blessed. In the same way, the blessings in your life that have come from your heritage are not to be viewed as symbols of superiority. They have been given to you so that you might bless the world with them.

Many of the Jews, especially the religious leaders, missed the point altogether. They thought that the label "God's chosen people" meant that they were better than all the other nations of the earth. Jesus revealed that God's love was toward all men, even the Samaritans and the Gentiles. The Jewish perception was so deeply ingrained that even Peter was uncertain as to whether or not Gentiles who had received the Holy Spirit could be baptized without first becoming Jews (Acts 10).

God does not prefer one race over another. If by His Spirit He lives in a redeemed people, it is unthinkable for them to say, "I and my race are superior." God is not a respecter of persons (Acts 10:34). An impartial God doesn't provide for one person a better life than He provides another simply because of his race. Neither does He designate one race to live more miserably than another.

There are groups of people whose oppressed status is the result of prejudice and racism. But God does not cause this victimization. It is the height of arrogance and hypocrisy to victimize a people-group, and then to declare that this was God's destiny for them. Such was the case with the theological justification many used to support the atrocities of apartheid, the Nazi holocaust, and slavery.

The Church's Charge

Jesus said, *"Go therefore and make disciples of all the nations, baptizing them in the name of the Father and the Son and the Holy Spirit, teaching them to observe all that I commanded you; and lo, I am with you always, even to the end of the age"* (Matt. 28:19–20 NAS). As previously mentioned, the word translated as "nation" is the Greek word *ethnos*, from which we get the English word "ethnic." Our commission is to make disciples of people of every national, ethnic, cultural, and racial group on earth. The obvious implication is that we are to do more than simply send a care package with a gospel tract in it. We are instructed to win them, baptize them, disciple them, teach them the full message of the gospel, and keep up the good work until the end of the age. Nothing could be clearer.

The very nature of the kingdom of God is diversity. The mission of the kingdom is the racial, national, and ethnic inclusion of all of mankind under the banner of Jesus Christ. You cannot be an ambassador of this kingdom and harbor prejudice or bigotry. Even an attitude of racial and ethnic *preference* puts you at odds with the express purpose of the kingdom.

How can you make disciples of people who are different from yourself if you're not willing to lay aside prejudice, preference, and an aversion to multiculturalism? Fulfilling the Great Commission requires sensitivity to and the accommodation of other cultures. We are to surrender our prejudices and preferences in order to reach people for Christ. The mere fact that the Great Commission is a command, not an option, infers that people with the Spirit of God living within them are innately qualified to share the gospel with diversified groups. Christians are charged to carry the gospel to the ends of the earth as cultural ambassadors.

Willingness to model diversity in our lives and in the local church is a dynamic testimony to the world. The trend of the 1980s and 1990s was for people to identify themselves "ethnocentrically." Consequently, the population is dividing into smaller and smaller groups. You might say we're becoming a world full of little gangs. To such a fragmented culture, the testimony of Jesus Christ is this: *I have saved Jews and Gentiles. I have saved slaves and the free; the strong and the weak. I have saved the intellectual, as well as those having no formal education. I have saved the rich and the poor; the black and the white. I have saved the Asian and the Hispanic; the Indians and other races of people.*

One good thing about the world becoming darker and darker spiritually is that it doesn't take a high-intensity flood light to get noticed. Even a candle will attract attention in a very dark place, unless it's hidden under a bushel basket. In a divisive world, all Christians have to do to make an extraordinary impact is simply to live and act like true Christians. If you love people with the love of Christ, regardless of their race, culture, or ethnic origin, then the world will be astounded. They will sit up and take notice, and will likely be more inclined to receive the gospel you have to share.

To fulfill the Great Commission, our hearts have to change. One pastor asked me, "Is it conceivable that the church can overcome this racial divisiveness, when the world we live in is filled with so many victimized people? Can we really achieve racial reconciliation?" I realized that if I said *no*, then I would be conceding that the gospel does not have the answers to our deepest personal and societal problems. So I quickly said *yes*, but with this qualification: Freeing people from the grip of hatred and leading them to become models of harmony is a tall order. It can be compared to a young boy attempting to tackle a professional football player.

Reconcilers are up against a real, live giant. But we cannot shy away from this modern-day Goliath. Like David, who faced his own Goliath many years ago, we have to say to ourselves, *It has to start with me!* If I don't begin to deal with the issues of reconciliation and restoration in my own soul, then I cannot assume these things will ever take place in anyone else's. In my obedience to Christ, I am compelled to take the necessary steps to change the world around me.

Similarly, your relationship with Christ, your life in the kingdom and your experience with the Holy Spirit living in you should cause your thinking to change. Once we recognize that our ideas are diametrically opposed to Christ and the nature of His kingdom, renewing our minds, conversation, and actions becomes the highest order of business. The battle must be fought in your heart as well as within your sphere of influence.

In August of 1992, an all-white jury acquitted four policemen on all but one count in the March 1991 beating of a black motorist, Rodney King. The African-American community was doubly offended, first by the act and then by the acquittal. When the riots occurred in South-Central Los Angeles following the first Rodney King verdict, it was as if someone injected our country with an antireconciliation virus.

Many people (both whites and blacks) could not understand why the citizens of South-Central Los Angeles vandalized and destroyed their own community. In no way do I condone their actions, but I understand the rioters' anger about the rank insensitivity American society had demonstrated toward the plight of an African-American.

Adopting cultural sensitivity toward others is no small task, especially in a society where we're constantly faced with the repercussions of prejudice. Nevertheless, I believe that in Christ we have the power to overcome sin and the evils of society. In Christ we have the opportunity to become one man.

——— *Chapter 5* ———

LOOKING IN THE MIRROR

My four o'clock counseling appointment was on time. Just the way I like it, punctual. As the Jamaican gentleman sat in my office, life's toil was evident on his face. I didn't know everything he was dealing with, but I did know he was struggling with being part of an interracial church.

"John," I asked, "what's troubling you?"

"Pastor, when I was eight years old, my house was firebombed. My two brothers and I were in our bedroom when we heard the sound of one of our windows shattering. Four Molotov cocktail bombs were thrown against the back of our house in an attempt to kill my family and destroy our home. You preach on racial reconciliation, but what about my victimization? Should I just forget the pain and agony, the many death threats we received, and the bombing of my home? Tell me, what does the Bible have to say to me, the victim of a hate crime?"

According to the articles he handed me on the case, six youths were caught and tried for arson, criminal conspiracy, criminal mischief, illegal possession of a dangerous instrument, and endangering the life of a minor. After being found guilty, they faced no jail time. Their only punishment was to pay fifty dollars each to John's family for the damage caused to the house. Before I could comment, John gave me a stack of letters his family had received following the incident. I knew

I had to read them because his healing could only begin when I, a Christian leader, understood his pain. One letter read:

> Dear _____ Family:
>
> This letter is being written to you in appreciation for the damages that were done to your home. I don't know why you all have to move into the beautiful white areas to live, as you turn them into slums anyway. I only wish that more niggers' homes were destroyed, as we can't seem to wipe you out. One comes in and before you know it, you are all here. I wish you would tell me why you want to move into white neighborhoods, or is it because you know that you're not wanted. Please move out; and until you do, you will be given no peace. I received your name and address from the news and I was happy to express my feelings toward you.

John said so many letters like this one had been sent to his home that the police had to keep an around-the-clock watch on the house. Thankfully, John admitted that a few positive letters had also come from people in the white community. One said:

> Dear Mr. and Mrs. _____:
>
> I have just read in tonight's "Press" the hateful, moronic and disgusting firebombing of your home. This thing (and I do mean "thing," like something that comes crawling and slobbering out of a murky marsh) stinks.
>
> The creatures that did this to you may have my "coloration" (only an accident of birth, pigment and history) but they are assuredly not "my kind." I reject them for the vermin they

are. I feel no personal guilt only shame for certain others of this tormented world, white and black, who commit these kinds of irresponsible [*sic*], immoral and heartless deeds.

I understand the material damage was slight, and I pray any damage to your morale and the happiness of your children was also minor. "Hang in" there. Don't "move." This is your home, your investment. Frustrate these animals.

A small check is enclosed just as a token of one citizen's moral support. It won't repair any damage to your home, lawn, or psyches; but it will buy some ice cream and cokes for your four kids. Give them a little "party," on me. Tell them "Whitey" bought it, so the youngsters won't grow up hating ALL whites.

That counseling session with John compelled me to revise my theology of cross-cultural ministry; from that day forward, my preaching became less about theory and more about practical, tangible lifestyle changes. Leading a multiracial church was not just fun and games. These were real people who had real problems. They needed real answers.

In *Mastering the Pastoral Role*, Ben Patterson writes, "The place God calls you to is the place where deep gladness and the world's deep hunger meet."[1] I was experiencing a genuine gladness that people were feeling open enough to speak with me about their uneasiness with racial issues. Yet I knew they were in real pain.

"I Never Felt So White Before"

One of the women in my congregation shared the following story with me as she groped to understand her dilemma. I have given the people fictitious names to protect their privacy, but the facts of this painful story are completely true.

As the Jensens, a Caucasian family, entered the sanctuary of a vibrant African-American evangelical church, the youth drama team was in the middle of a dramatic presentation. They were good—very good. Betty Jensen turned to the gentleman standing next to her at the back of the church, smiled, and said, "Praise the Lord!" Instead of giving a friendly response, he glared at her and returned her greeting with an icy silence. A bitter chill suddenly engulfed her.

Sally, a young African-American woman who had become a dear friend and an integral part of the Jensen family, was preparing to minister in song. She called out to Betty, "Mom, where are my accompaniment tracks?" The three black women sitting nearest Sally wrenched their necks around and shot disgusted looks, as if to say, *What do you mean, calling that white woman, "Mom"?*

Betty had never felt so white in all her life. The Jensen family had been invited to attend this youth convention. The only information they had been given was the time, place, date, and directions to the church. So there they were—a Spirit-filled Christian family, including an Italian father, an Irish mother, their daughter, and a spiritually adopted African-American daughter—in an all-black congregation. It had never occurred to them to question whether the youth convention would be white, black, Asian, or Hispanic. The Jensen family was there to celebrate the lordship of Jesus Christ with people of like faith.

"I never knew that in God's house, among brothers and sisters, our hearts could be held so tightly in the hammerlock of prejudice," Betty told me. For months later, in her multiracial home church (Christ Church), Betty searched each face and every "godly" embrace for hidden hostility.

The icy silence, mean stares, and disgusted looks the black congregation had aimed at Betty communicated the message, "Whitey,
what are you doing in our church?" Instead of being uplifted in the
house of God, Betty left that meeting with fear, alienation, and shock
over the unexpected incident.

As she related her experience to me, I simply conveyed to her that
racism is a real problem in the local church. I told her that although her
episode was blatant and overt, most often such incidents are subtle and
unnoticeable. Whether the victimization is black-to-white or white-to-
black, the church of Jesus Christ suffers when ignorance and racial
prejudice rear their ugly heads.

Jesus' Great Commission, *"Go therefore and make disciples of
all the nations..."* (Matt. 28:19 NAS), is jeopardized by racists within the
Christian faith, no matter how privately or passively these people maintain their biases. To preach Christ in our society, we cannot ignore the
reality of racism. For far too long, Christianity has been accused of
being out of touch and irrelevant to the current needs of society. To
ignore the problem of schisms in the body of Christ is to spurn the call
of the Great Commission.

The renowned preacher and author John R. W. Stott addressed
the subject of relevance as follows:

A few years ago I was talking with two students who were
brothers, one at Oxford University and the other at
Edinburgh. They had been brought up in a traditional Christian home, both their parents being practicing Christians.
But now they had renounced their parents' faith and their
Christian upbringing. One was a complete atheist, he told
me; the other preferred to call himself an agnostic. What
happened? I asked. Was it that they no longer believed

Christianity to be true? "No," they replied, "that's not our problem. We're not really interested to know whether Christianity is true. And if you were able to convince us that it is, we're not at all sure we would embrace it." "What is your problem, then?" I asked with some astonishment. "What we want to know," they went on, "is not whether Christianity is *true*, but whether it's *relevant*."[2]

To move ahead in becoming world-class Christians, we must search our souls for purity. James' letter points to the reality that true religion can only stem from examining yourself by looking intently into the perfect law—the mirror of the Word of God (James 1:23–25).

LOOKING IN THE MIRROR

Racism certainly isn't a new problem in society. But whether it's displayed overtly as our history proves, or privately and subtly as is often the case today, racism is always a deadly poison. It breeds hatred, anger, and suspicion. Victims of racism feel discouraged and hopeless. And the sin of hatred eats away at the consciences of the abusers. This demonic combination lessens the dignity and quality of life of both groups.

The painful issue that many "saints" want to ignore or deny today is that racism exists in the church. Yes, in the church! It's been said that eleven o'clock on Sunday morning is the most racist hour in America. In 1990, the George Barna Research Group documented that most American churches (79 percent) were composed of attendees of the same race.[3]

Barna's survey resulted in three conclusions regarding the racial composition of American churches (Table 1). First, 79 percent of all congregations are monoracial. Second, 18 percent of churches have 1 to 10 percent of their congregants coming from races other than the majority. And third, 3 percent of churches have 11 percent or more parishioners of a race different from that of the majority of the congregation.

It must be noted that the racial makeup of American churches is not a conclusive indication that these congregations are prejudiced. However, if most church attendees are going to houses of worship that cater only to people of their own race, at the very least, they have a problem of spiritual alienation from large segments of the body of Christ. We will discover in chapters 6 and 7 that social estrangement is one of the by-products of prejudice.

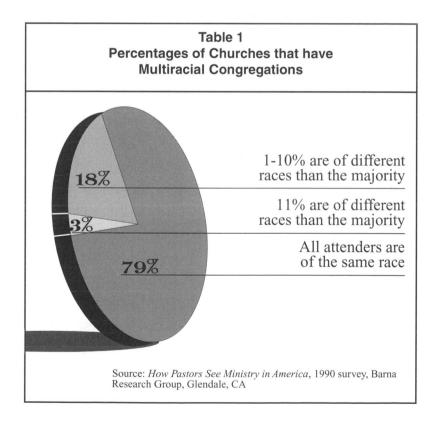

Table 1
Percentages of Churches that have
Multiracial Congregations

18%

3%

79%

1-10% are of different races than the majority

11% are of different races than the majority

All attenders are of the same race

Source: *How Pastors See Ministry in America*, 1990 survey, Barna Research Group, Glendale, CA

Racism can be considered a deadly poison because it spreads throughout society, the church, and wherever it is allowed to exist. Like a poisonous contaminant that is introduced into someone's system, racism causes the vital organs of society or the church to stop functioning as God intended. The challenge we face is how to apply an antidote to correct the problem before a global disaster occurs.

THE EFFECTS OF RACISM ON SOCIETY

In the preceding true stories, racism played a significant role in the choices each person (whether the abused or the abuser) made. The choice made by the Jamaican black family to live in a predominantly white neighborhood resulted in the family's house being firebombed. Most minorities don't wake up one morning saying, "Gee, we want to live in an all-white neighborhood." People usually purchase the best homes they can afford in communities that offer the most to their families. In most cases, it's the schools, the churches, convenience to work, and the future value of their investment that attract a minority family to a given neighborhood—not the racial composition of the area.

In the case of the Jamaican family, the acts of violence and prejudice against them hurt financially, emotionally, and psychologically. The physical damage to their home also had to be repaired. Had the perpetrators of this heinous crime not been caught, the family and its insurance company would have had to absorb all of the expenses. As you know, there's usually a hefty deductible on homeowners' insurance. Thus, in addition to living in constant fear of further violence, these victims were forced to reach into their pockets to pay for a portion of the damage. Racial hatred has a devastating financial effect on its victims.

Individual states, such as my home state of New Jersey, are passing laws to increase the penalties for so-called "hate crimes." The government cannot enforce harmony, but it can send the message that bigotry and hatred will not be tolerated. Specifically, a new law referred to as the Ethnic Intimidation Act allows the victims of racially motivated crimes to sue for damages, such as medical and counseling fees, lost time at work, emotional distress, attorneys' fees, and punitive damages. The state may also litigate on the victim's behalf. Under this law, victims gained further rights in that "parents and guardians of the abuser also can be liable for penalties if their conduct contributed to their child's bias [*sic*] actions."[4] Although the motives of many politicians in enacting the new law were self-serving and politically based, the policy is still of benefit to society.

In Oregon, the family of an Ethiopian immigrant murdered by a group of "racist skinheads" won a $12.5 million verdict against the white supremacist group. In Chicago, a Jewish family won a $1.8 million verdict against neighbors who conducted an extended anti-Semitic campaign.[5] Since hate crimes cause great damage, both emotional and financial, the courts are saying "pay up." It must be noted that though there is an increased awareness of the costs of hate crimes, the percentage of unpaid victims far outweighs the few victims who've received hefty settlements.

Real crimes of hatred have placed a heavy financial load on society (not just the victims), totaling countless millions of dollars each year. A portion of the tax dollars originating from hardworking citizens is apportioned to federal and state organizations annually for handling racially motivated crimes. Salaried employees are hired to manage government agencies such as the Department of Public Safety. Former President Bush felt compelled to offer a $19 million program to fight crime and foster education in selected inner-city neighborhoods. According to *U.S. News and World Report*, the 1992 riots stemming from the miscarriage of justice associated with the racially motivated beating of Rodney King left South-Central Los Angeles with an estimated $1 billion in damages, more than fifty dead, and 2,300 injured.[6]

I'm certainly not against the formation of these government organizations, nor do I question their roles in society. My point is that because of the poison of racism, needless tax dollars are distributed to such watchdog groups to protect and care for victims. The data supporting the assertion that racism puts a significant financial strain on society is indisputable. The more pertinent issue is the intangible price paid by the victims of such crimes. The cost of repairing the physical damage associated with racist acts cannot be compared to the cost of healing the psychological trauma stemming from this unwarranted invasion of hatred.

THE EFFECTS OF RACISM ON THE CHURCH

The church is composed of people at every stage of spiritual growth. Therefore, the church will face every moral and social problem to some extent or another. As a vital part of society, the church functions to communicate the mind of God to the consciences of unchurched humanity. Nevertheless, a percentage of church members originate from the crowd of bigots, racists, and culturally inept people. The old mannerisms, preferences, and biases of these people accompany them into the church.

Paul wrote to the church at Corinth about its members' inability to get along with each other. After citing a long list of unholy characteristics, he wrote, *"And such were some of you; but you were washed, but you were sanctified, but you were justified in the name of the Lord*

Jesus Christ, and in the Spirit of our God" (1 Cor. 6:11 NAS). God removes the guilt and shame of what we were before salvation. It is true that "whosoever will may come," including bigots, racists, and so forth. But you cannot come into Christ's kingdom still clinging to the sins for which Christ died to deliver us.

While it is true that prejudice is being introduced to the church via new converts, it's also true that prejudice comes into the church through the blatant cultural and racial unfamiliarity of the young ministers produced by our evangelical seminaries. David Claerbaut writes:

> Then as that [white] child reaches adulthood and plans, perhaps, to go into Christian ministry, he attends a Christian college with a largely white faculty, staff, and student body, finally to finish in a white middle-class seminary that tries to prepare him for working with all kinds of people. If by then he is not to some extent a purveyor of racism and prejudice, it would be rather surprising, for all agree that a person's environment is a major influence on his attitudes, values, beliefs, and behaviors.[7]

Dr. David Hubbard, president of Fuller Theological Seminary, made a similar observation in an interview with *Christianity Today*:

> During the L.A. riots, a student gave a poignant word when she stood in a convocation and said, "I am being prepared at Fuller to minister in a church that I do not attend." That was important for us to hear. Here's an African-American woman who's attending a church in which we are not preparing her to minister.[8]

Racism and cultural ignorance have entered the church from many different sources. The mission of the church is to "make disciples" of people and to "teach them" to observe Christ's commands. When the church as a whole tolerates separatism, how can anyone expect the seeds of prejudice to be eradicated from its individual members?

The phenomenon known as "white flight" supports the premise that prejudice does indeed exist in the evangelical church, and it hampers the fulfillment of the Lord's command to go and make disciples of all nations. "White flight" is a term used to describe the quiet migration of Caucasians (white churches included) from urban to suburban communities. The once all-white urban neighborhoods of these congregations have changed rapidly due to the influx of minorities to the cities. Rather than reshaping the message of the gospel to fit the context of their new, nonwhite neighborhoods, these congregations have picked up and moved away.

It could be said that churches move to the suburbs only because they are following the migration of their members. But the mission and strategic plan of the church is what truly influences every building program. In short, the location of the church is determined by the designated target membership (i.e., the group of people the church wants to attract, as opposed to those they either don't want or on whom they place a lower priority). When those God brings to the church's doorstep are not wanted, some churches simply move the doorstep. When you consider the effort and expense of moving, you can see the power and pervasiveness of prejudice in the evangelical and mainline denominational churches.

The Effects of Racism on the Person

The effect of racism on the church is a real one. Each church should rethink its ministry policies in order to develop a more inclusive approach. Without a commitment to clear reconciliatory teaching and a willingness to change our views, the Great Commission will become an unreachable or perhaps even undesired goal for the church.

A dear friend once confided to me that during her adolescent years she wished she were black, not white. She had concluded that because the black race was so heavily oppressed, they must be special to the Lord, since He too was a victim. As a child born into a dysfunctional family, she had experienced a painful life. It was difficult for her to believe that God actually loved her. Consequently, she felt that to be dear to Jesus, she needed to be black. Typically we hear the opposite feelings from people of color. The poison of racism produces a lot of strange thinking patterns.

Aberrant theological views are created to offer "healing and camaraderie" to the victims. For example, in the late 1980s and early 1990s, a noticeable number of black churches in America began espousing a teaching called "the message of the Cushites." The word *cush* is Hebrew for "black," "burnt face," or "dark skin." Scripture signifies that the black race stemmed from Noah's grandson, Cush. On the surface, the Cushite Movement was a cry for justice and equality in the Christian world. However, it had a strong undercurrent of anger, bitterness, and separatism.

Because of the weakness and brevity of the movement, it is almost impossible to find literature on the subject today. It's important to note that few blacks embraced the teaching because of its divisive nature. However, we cannot ignore the real pain that our black Christian brothers and sisters are facing because of a "lily-white gospel" and the inaccurate portrayal of Jesus as a blond-haired, blue-eyed Anglo-Saxon. Similarly, black churches are losing many young people to the philosophies of the Black Muslims and other separatist groups because these teachings offer them a way to deal with the injustices of racism.

In their quest to heal the sin of prejudice, partisans of the Cushite Movement, Black Muslims, and other such groups have turned to a one-sided view of Scripture. But the indictment should not be leveled against them alone. Rather, it should be handed to the larger portion of the body of Christ in America (predominantly Caucasian), which sits idly by and watches victimized blacks try to heal themselves of the massive spiritual attack called racism.

Here's the $64,000 question: Is the church prepared to look herself squarely in the mirror, or will she continue to give lip-service to the idea of reconciliation until Christ returns?

—— Chapter 6 ——

ARE YOU COMFORTABLE AROUND ME?

The ills of prejudice are commonplace in modern society. The church has not been immune to this social disease, which has done so much damage throughout history. In the present day, Christians are being forced to identify the presence of prejudice, contemplate the appropriate biblical response, and take practical steps to achieve true reconciliation. I realize that establishing racial harmony is not an easy task. It's difficult enough to get people of different races to agree on a suitable definition of the word *prejudice*, much less to get them to agree upon a solution. Nevertheless, the church must carry out her mission to model racial unity both inside and outside the parish walls. In a divided society, only the church can model unity. Congregations that are sensitive to how the Holy Spirit deals with their biases must trumpet this sentiment throughout their spheres of influence.

THE MEANING OF PREJUDICE

The word *prejudice* originated from the Latin noun *praejudicium*, which means "a previous judgment or damage." The English word means "an adverse judgment or opinion formed beforehand or without knowledge or examination of the facts."[1] In defining the term, *Webster's Ninth New Collegiate Dictionary* indicates that it is more than just a passive prejudgment, but hostility: "an irrational attitude of hostility directed against an individual, a group, a race, or their supposed characteristics."[2] *The New English Dictionary* offers positive and negative shades of meaning: "A feeling, favorable or unfavorable, toward a person or thing, prior to, or not based on, actual experience."[3]

Although the word *prejudice* can refer to prejudging either positively or negatively, most definitions focus on the unwarranted negative conclusions reached because of a faulty judgment of another. A more technical, behavioral definition was presented by sociologist Dr. Gordon Allport in *The Nature of Prejudice*. Allport writes that prejudice is "an avertive or hostile attitude toward a person who belongs to a group, simply because he belongs to that group, and is therefore presumed to have objectionable qualities ascribed to the group."[4]

This definition indicates that a prejudiced individual makes a calculated decision to avoid interaction with people of a certain group. Prior to any dealings with an individual member of that group, an unwarranted negative idea is formulated about him or her. This idea has nothing to do with the person's character or actions, but exists simply because he or she is a member of a particular group.

These definitions merely reflect what we all should know by natural reasoning—that prejudice is demeaning to those who harbor it, devastating to the victims of it, and divisive to society. In an organization, society, or nation divided by prejudice, all sides lose. A prejudiced body always deteriorates spiritually and morally until it descends into chaos. Indeed, Jesus said, *"If a house is divided against itself, that house cannot stand"* (Mark 3:25).

Surprisingly, some misguided people have tried to soften the meaning of the word *prejudice* by applying a false concept of mercy to it.

Assuming that prejudice is simply one's preference is an attempt to cushion and condone it. Although this excuse may be palatable, emotional and sometimes physical damage is done to victims of prejudice.

The word *preference* suggests a morally neutral choice to interact with certain individuals because they are the ones who give you pleasure or stimulate your thinking. "Preference" does not imply improper ethical or moral behavior. But the downside of choosing not to socialize with a certain group is that negative prejudices will naturally emerge toward that group. Preferential choices are not unethical if the reason for discrimination relates to something that should be avoided such as bad character or convictions.

Another fallacy that must be addressed is that prejudice is actually born out of ignorance. Quite obviously, ignorance about another race can fuel divisiveness and foster all kinds of false opinions. But the notion that knowledge is the remedy to prejudice is not necessarily true! Allport's research confirms that an irrational attitude of hostility is not caused solely by a lack of knowledge. Prejudice, then, is not equated with ignorance. He formulates his thesis around the idea that prejudice contains two essential ingredients: 1) There must be an attitude of favor or disfavor; and, 2) it must be related to an overgeneralized judgment.

According to Allport, "A prejudice, unlike a misconception, is actively resistant to all evidence that would unseat it. We tend to grow emotional when a prejudice is threatened with contradiction. Thus the difference between ordinary prejudgments and prejudice is that one can discuss and rectify a prejudgment without emotional resistance."[5] So information alone will not serve as an adequate solution to prejudice. If it would, a presentation of the facts about another group would cure any deliberate social alienation. Education alone is not sufficient in combating bigotry. It should only be viewed as one of the many steps to healing this social disease.

To illustrate my point, David was a Korean boy who thought that all Hispanics were academically inferior to Asians. Had this been a prejudgment based only on ignorance, it easily could have been erased by the facts. But after graduating from the sixth grade, David was placed in a seventh grade class with five Hispanic students whose grades were considerably higher than his. David thought to himself, *There's no way these people are smarter than I am. They must have cheated on all the exams!*

New information did not change David's original notion. He simply maneuvered himself around the facts to maintain ownership of his original misconception. Obviously, knowledge is not the only weapon needed to combat racism.

THE REAL DEFINITION OF RACISM

Prejudice by any name, be it preference, ignorance, or another label, results in an entire group of unique individuals being devalued—limited in terms of the opportunities afforded them, their perceived potential, and most of all, their self-worth. Many times such overgeneralized judgments are formed solely on unsubstantiated, circumstantial information, without any personal contact with an individual from that group. Other times these prejudicial beliefs and attitudes are formed toward an entire cultural, ethnic, or racial group based on only a few personal experiences—possibly, from only one encounter. When groups become socially alienated from one another, an invisible tension eventually leads to more exaggerated false perceptions that increase racial intolerance.

Washington and Kehrein, in their book *Breaking Down Walls*, indicate that various races have different working definitions of the word *racism*.

When African-Americans use the term racism, the word covers a broad spectrum. Any action on the part of whites that is different because it is directed at a black person can be racist....For instance, to assume that a black man wearing surgical scrubs and walking through a hospital corridor is an orderly and not a doctor—that's racist....But white people use the word racism for only extreme actions. They agree that when the Ku Klux Klan burns a cross on a person's lawn or threatens a lynching, that's racist....Actions short of that, however, typically are labeled in graduated terms from *bigotry* down to *misinterpretation.*[6]

Although the authors only viewed the connotation of racism from an African-American and a Caucasian perspective, people of every race interpret this word based on the experiences of their own lives and from the related experiences of their friends and family.

LEVELS OF PREJUDICE

There are also different levels of prejudice. Dr. Allport concluded that there are five significant degrees to which people act out their prejudice. These actions range from talking about it with friends, to avoiding a certain group, to discriminatory actions (such as excluding all members of a group from social privileges, employment opportunities, or housing), to physically attacking members of the group, and finally, to extermination of the group (i.e., massacres, lynchings, ethnic cleansings, and so on).[7]

These levels point to the fact that prejudice never remains a private issue. Whether it's simply making prejudicial comments to your friends or joining a lynch mob, eventually you will begin acting out your secret thoughts. Since anger and distrust are by-products of prejudice, it stands to reason that you will graduate from one level of action to another. The increasing number of hate crimes committed each year is a sign that this very progression is taking place. It's easy to overlook the potential danger of the milder, nonviolent forms of prejudice, but these are rooted in the same attitudes that are behind physical attacks and barbaric ethnic cleansing.

For example, the racist acts of the Ku Klux Klan appear more damaging to our country than the subtle distrust a person might have of someone of another race. Consequently, when someone exhibits a milder form of racism his friends rarely notice the depth of prejudice. Only through confrontation, direct interaction with someone of another race, or divine revelation from the Spirit of God is someone made aware of this problem in his or her life.

The general populace considers blatant forms of racism as heinous crimes. Even the most sinful heathens who are living in open disobedience and rebellion toward God's laws find large-scale racially motivated crimes to be barbaric and unjustifiable. For example, the anti-Semitic war crimes performed against Jews in Hitler's Nazi Germany have received universal condemnation. However, secret feelings of prejudice held against a neighbor underscore a smaller, yet potentially explosive problem. If left unchecked, this quiet social distrust can evolve into violence of a catastrophic order.

OLD TESTAMENT PREJUDICE

Noted sociologists such as Dr. Kenneth Clark have concluded from their studies that racism is the product of one's environment.[8] I agree that the perpetuation of racism is nurtured by environment and culture.

But prejudice and the racism it produces are clearly social evils created by personal sin. Their root cause can be traced to the fall of mankind, which resulted from the sin of Adam. Paul concluded that Adam's sin had generational implications: *"Wherefore, as by one man sin entered into the world, and death by sin; and so death passed upon all men, for that all have sinned"* (Rom. 5:12 KJV). Because the roots of racism entered the world in the beautiful Garden of Eden, it now plagues the world as a thorn bush of life.

Although the word *prejudice* is not used specifically in the Bible, vivid examples of it are recorded. Not only was it present in certain eras, but some of the most influential characters in Scripture were found to be infected with prejudice. The Scriptures record how God dealt with this sin in the days of Moses, Jeremiah, Jesus, and the early church.

Miriam and Aaron spoke out against their brother, Moses, for marrying a Cushite (a dark-skinned or black) woman (Num. 12:1–16). Whether the controversy stirred up by Miriam and Aaron was over a racial or a religious difference is a well-debated theological issue. The fact of the matter is that either reason points to a form of prejudice. Even religious intolerance (that is, taking a stand for what you believe) should not be handled in a bitter or disrespectful way. God became angry and showed His displeasure by striking Miriam with leprosy.

In Jeremiah's attempt to prophesy a clear word to rebellious Israel about the nation's need to practice a lifestyle of holiness, he illustrated his point by asking, *"Can the Ethiopian change his skin...? Then you also can do good who are accustomed to do evil"* (Jer. 13:23 NAS). The prophets often spoke for God by drawing from the expressions and clichés most familiar to their hearers. God's wisdom is obvious in this practice; He wants people to clearly understand His concerns through the prophetic utterance. God does not want His people to make an excuse of the language barrier and continue in their disobedience.

The skin color of the Ethiopians probably did raise the question in many minds: *Why are those people dark skinned? Can their skin color be changed?* Jokes, inferences, and prejudicial conclusions probably existed in the Jewish community about the skin pigmentation of the Ethiopians. And, most likely, the Ethiopians had their own thoughts about the skin color of other ethnic groups. Jeremiah's reference to the inability to change skin color infers that some people of that era may have thought that another skin pigmentation was better or more socially acceptable than that of the Ethiopian. Jeremiah's prophetic word not only called the Hebrews to repentance, but it also illustrates to us how the black race may have been viewed during that period in history.

PREJUDICE IN THE EARLY CHURCH

The sixth chapter of Acts opens with the discovery of the social disease of prejudice spreading throughout the membership of the church at Jerusalem:

> *Now at this time while the disciples were increasing in number, a complaint arose on the part of the Hellenistic Jews against the native Hebrews, because their widows were being overlooked in the daily serving of food.* (Acts 6:1 NAS)

This dispute had to do with the care of elderly widows. The early church was deeply moved by the needs of widows. It was a common practice to provide for widows who were active members of a congregation. The apostle Paul relayed his concerns about this matter to his spiritual son, Timothy. According to Paul, a widow who qualified for church assistance had to be at least sixty years old and have no living relatives who could provide for her. Her character and reputation had to be impeccable. Her hope and faith in God had to be settled issues, verifiable through a daily lifestyle of prayer and intercession (1 Tim. 5:3–16). Although Paul's admonition was given several decades after the events in Acts, it reflects a tradition that existed from the very beginning of the church.

The philosophy of ministry practiced by the early church was that any service performed by one member to another was a significant activity that ultimately led to the building up of the community. The duty performed was an act of grace, carried out vicariously on the Lord's behalf. The act of "waiting on tables" (Acts 6:2) was directly linked to the service of love Christians demonstrated visibly toward one another at the common meals. When this attitude of unselfish love was not being demonstrated, it became apparent that something was wrong and needed to be corrected.

In Acts 6:1, a distinction was made between the two types of widows being served. This is evidenced by the fact that a complaint *arose* against the Hebraic Jews from the Hellenistic Jews. They said that the Hellenistic widows were being *overlooked* in the daily serving of food. The word *arose* has to do with "a continual growing." Evidently, the frustration voiced at that moment represented a mounting concern on the part of the Hellenistic Jews. It is likely that some event had caused the problem to come to the fore.

The word *overlooked* connotes feelings of disregard and neglect. The Hebrews were accused of willfully disregarding and neglecting the Hellenistic widows in the distribution of daily sustenance. This is a very strong accusation!

The emotional upheaval of rejection leaves a person feeling unwanted and unwelcome. Prejudice produces rejection of the highest order. When a person is consistently overlooked, he or she cannot help but feel deeply wounded and rejected. It's a terrible feeling! And if this kind of rejection occurs within the kingdom of God, where else can one turn? Jesus asked Peter, *"You do not want to go away also, do you?"* Peter responded, *"Lord, to whom shall we go? You have words of eternal life"* (John 6:67–68 NAS). In the body of Christ, we have no place else to turn.

Wealthy individuals in the early church divided up their estates. The proceeds were shared with others based upon their needs. The early church in Jerusalem lived a communal lifestyle. In communal living, if someone in the community is not having his emotional needs addressed, his only alternative is to go outside the community for help. The church is a community, but not just any type of community. It is a place for God-fearing, God-loving, Spirit-transformed people. When this community offers no healing or is insensitive to another's hurts, pains, frailties, and struggles, this is a grave indictment against the Christian experience. This is the problem faced by the Jerusalem church.

Let's take a closer look at the differences between the two Jewish factions involved in the altercation. F. F. Bruce comments that the Hellenists were Jews living in Jerusalem who were chiefly distinguished by reading the Scriptures and worshipping at the synagogue only in Greek.[9]

On the other hand, Hebraic Jews considered themselves pure and undefiled. They felt that keeping strict allegiance to the language and customs of their fathers made them more historically accurate in representing what it meant to be Jewish. Consequently, as the image of self-importance and self-righteousness grew in the minds of the Hebraic Jews, they became prejudiced, and the Hellenistic Jews were disregarded.

Think about the plight of the widows. With no one to take care of them, they were trapped by their financial situation. The church came alongside them and promised assistance. Yet the very community that offered healing also victimized them. Prejudice does indeed hurt! Individuals who have been hurt, maimed, and crippled by society look to the church for healing, not added grief.

The tension between the two Jewish groups is a type of the tension that exists in the larger body of Christ today. Though we may be different—racially, culturally and ethnically—we still have a common link to our spiritual heritage. Becoming a Christian doesn't mean you forget your culture or ethnicity. Note that it was not the Hebraic Jews who were concerned about equity in the Christian community, nor was it the Hellenistic widows themselves. It was the Hellenistic, non-Palestinian Jews who were sensitive to the condition of the widows. These believers shed light on the issue, and it was addressed.

Experiencing salvation did not make the members of either cultural group ignorant of their historical or visible differences. Salvation should make us more self-aware in a constructive, Christ-glorifying way. The Jerusalem church, in its early stages, had to deal head-on with cultural prejudice. Serious students of the Bible cannot deny the existence of the problem! God gave the apostles wisdom and courage to fight it. They acknowledged its existence and chose seven leaders with exemplary character traits who could provide the objectivity needed to solve this major social problem.

As Christians, we cannot behave like ostriches, sticking our heads in a hole and expecting the hurts and bruises of life to simply go away. We have a responsibility—a moral one—to exemplify racial reconciliation in our spheres of influence. Fear is one of the primary reasons why many church leaders and congregations don't even mention (much less teach on) subjects like sex, divorce, incest, and prejudice. As a consequence, many hurting people walk away thinking there are no answers in the house of God for such problems. Yet others interpret this silence to mean that certain words are taboo—that is, words like *racism*, *bigot*, and *rape* should not be spoken in church, lest some heavenly-minded saint be offended.

Most congregations and congregational leaders are living in such perilous denial of prejudice and racism that they present no biblical answers to current social ills. If parishioners don't understand what the Bible has to say about the everyday problems people face in the real world, they will be forced to turn to the world for answers. It's sad but true that worldly solutions don't have the redemptive qualities worth passing on to the next generation. For this reason, the phrase bears repeating: In a divided society, only the church can model unity.

Chapter 7

WHO IS MY NEIGHBOR?

P astor, I'm gonna be very honest with you. Do you remember the last meeting at our church's conference last year? Well, the conference committee had asked all of those who wanted prayer to come to the altar, where one of the speakers would pray for them. Pastor, in my heart, there was one speaker I did not want to go to for prayer. You see, I'd never had a Hispanic man lay hands on me and pray. But the way the ushers moved everyone toward the altar area, I found myself, a white man, standing in front of that Hispanic minister, requesting that he pray for me. I was extremely uncomfortable and awkward. Never before that night, Pastor, did I think of myself as being racially prejudiced."

Statements like these may seem unlikely coming from a Christian. Yet this was part of a real conversation that took place between a pastor friend of mine and a member of his congregation. The pastor later told me that he responded to his parishioner with mixed feelings. Even he was shocked to know that one of his members felt this way about people. Sobered by the thought that he had never taught on racial reconciliation, he also realized that there was no visible model in his congregation of an appreciation for diversity. There were no multiracial pictures or flags from various nations, nor was there a diversity of races on the platform in this church.

I was reminded of the subtlety of prejudice as I discussed the issues surrounding urban ministry and racially integrated churches with another pastor. "It was the local news that made me realize how much I was battling with prejudice," the pastor said. "I began to be conscious of how selectively I responded to the usual menu of bad news. A brutal killing would initially grab by attention. But if I saw that the victim was a person of a different race, my attention quickly faded. After all, it wasn't someone I knew, and it didn't happen in my neighborhood." Then he added, "As subtle as that may seem, it made me realize that some things in my heart and attitude had to change."

How do you know if you're prejudiced? When you get around people who are different from you, do you get tense? Do you act differently around certain groups of people? Are you uneasy or afraid? Is it that way with all people who are different from you or just with a certain group? Is your attention focused primarily on your differences or on the things you have in common?

It's not uncommon for people of different races to pass on the street and not speak or even glance at each other. Perhaps you've been guilty of this because you noticed a person's skin color out of the corner of your eye and quickly concluded that you need not speak to him. He wasn't in your peer group, was not a potential friend, and probably wasn't one of your neighbors or someone with whom you wanted to network. He might have been a part of your community, but not a part of your personal world. Consequently, there was no good reason to make contact. As insignificant as a passing acknowledgment may seem, such an action is often the best barometer of your attitude.

Who Is My Neighbor?

The Good Samaritan

Jesus regularly confronted people who sincerely considered themselves to be free of certain sins. He often helped them see where they
had missed the mark by using word pictures, such as the parable of the
Good Samaritan.

> 25*And behold, a certain lawyer stood up and put [Jesus] to
> the test, saying, "Teacher, what shall I do to inherit eternal
> life?" * 26*And He said to him, "What is written in the Law?
> How does it read to you?" * 27*And he answered and said,
> "YOU SHALL LOVE THE LORD YOUR GOD WITH ALL YOUR HEART, AND
> WITH ALL YOUR SOUL, AND WITH ALL YOUR STRENGTH, AND WITH ALL
> YOUR MIND; AND YOUR NEIGHBOR AS YOURSELF."*

> 28*And He said to him, "You have answered correctly; DO
> THIS, AND YOU WILL LIVE." * 29*But wishing to justify himself, he
> said to Jesus, "And who is my neighbor?"*

> 30*Jesus replied and said, "A certain man was going down from
> Jerusalem to Jericho; and he fell among robbers, and they
> stripped him and beat him, and went off leaving him half dead.*

> 31*And by chance a certain priest was going down on that road,
> and when he saw him, he passed by on the other side.*
> 32*And likewise a Levite also, when he came to the place and
> saw him, passed by on the other side.*

> 33*But a certain Samaritan, who was on a journey, came upon
> him; and when he saw him, he felt compassion, * 34*and came*

to him, and bandaged up his wounds, pouring oil and wine on them; and he put him on his own beast, and brought him to an inn, and took care of him. ³⁵*And on the next day he took out two denarii and gave them to the innkeeper and said, 'Take care of him; and whatever more you spend, when I return, I will repay you.'*

³⁶*Which of these three do you think proved to be a neighbor to the man who fell into the robbers' hands?"* ³⁷*And he said, "The one who showed mercy toward him." And Jesus said to him, "Go and do the same."* (Luke 10:25–37 NAS)

The story of the Good Samaritan is one of the best known of all the parables of Jesus. The term "good Samaritan" has long been an English colloquialism used by people who often have no idea who the Samaritans were or the story from which the term came. But the story should be well known in the church because of the fundamental principles it contains about living in the kingdom as a follower of Jesus.

First, the background of the characters and the setting must be discussed. The Samaritans were hated by the Jews for a variety of reasons that went back hundreds of years. Until the rise of the Assyrian Empire, Samaria was inhabited by the descendants of Israel, namely, the tribes of Ephraim and Manasseh. In those days, the tribes of Israel were divided into the northern kingdom, Israel, and the southern kingdom, Judah. When the Assyrians conquered Israel in 722 B.C., many were led into captivity and were replaced by foreign colonists who intermarried with the Israelites. Their descendants, who took on the name of the Samaritan region, were considered by the Jews to be half-breeds, having been polluted by foreign blood.

Their descendants, the Samaritans who remained in the territory of Israel during the Babylonian captivity, offered to help Zerubbabel and the Israelites who returned to rebuild the temple in Jerusalem. But Zerubbabel categorically rejected their help. Later, Ezra commanded all the Israelite men who had married Samaritan women to divorce their "pagan" wives (Ezra 10:1–4). Consequently, the Samaritans were again offended and wound up as allies of those who opposed the Jews, as well as of those who opposed the rebuilding of the temple and the city.

The Samaritans, who were descendants of Israel but who now were segregated and alienated from the rest of the Jews, asserted that Shechem, rather than Zion, was the true *beth el* or house of God. Shechem, of course, was located in Samaria. Consequently, the Samaritans had built a temple of their own on Mount Gerizim. Remember that the first question the woman at the well in the Samaritan village had asked Jesus dealt with which mountain was the appropriate place to worship (John 4:20).

The three most important aspects of a Jewish man's Hebrew identity were: 1) that he was a pure descendant of Abraham through Isaac, the child of the covenant promise; 2) that he worshipped at the temple in Jerusalem; and, 3) that he was a keeper of the Law. The Samaritans accepted only the Torah, the first five books of the Old Testament, and occasionally their scribes would change the wording in the Torah to suggest that Mount Gerizim was the authentic place of worship. Imagine how this horrified and offended the Jews!

Thus, the Samaritans were an offense to the Jews on each of these three points. They were also opportunists, who claimed they were Israelites when the Jews were in favor, and disassociated themselves when they were not.[1] The Jews and the Samaritans were the Hatfields and McCoys of the ancient world. Every generation collected its own list of offenses, and they fought like cats and dogs.

There have been countless sermons, articles, and commentaries written on the parable of the Good Samaritan. Though the insights and applications are endless, I want to highlight just a few aspects of the story.

Excuses Get Very Complicated.

First-century lawyers, like their modern counterparts, were experts at finding loopholes that allowed them to escape the straightforward commands of God. In doing so, they added to the already burgeoning system of legalistic interpretations among the Jews. The lawyers in Jesus' day (also called *scribes*) were experts on the Law of Moses and had created long, complicated interpretations of every aspect of the Law. In doing so, they had wandered away from its original intent and had missed the point altogether. In many cases, their interpretations were given for no other reason than to circumvent the Law of God. In this particular case, the lawyer did not ask Jesus to define "neighbor" simply because he was curious. The lawyer had already worked out his answer, which was undoubtedly long and complicated. The answer would also have been tailored to excuse him from the simple mandate to love his neighbor.

You can reduce the conflicts Jesus had with the scribes and Pharisees to this: He simply embraced the truth and rejected the creation of complex reasons and regulations that served only to justify sin and disobedience. When you step back and listen to all the excuses people use to justify their prejudice today, it actually sounds very comical.

The commands of God are very simple. "Love God and love your neighbor," Jesus said. The implication was that since this was the essence of the Law, by simply walking in love, you would automatically fulfill all of the Law. When you apply Christ's command to love your neighbor as yourself to questions of, racially divided churches, integrated schools, and the struggles of minorities in the inner city, how simple is your answer? If you have a dozen qualifying footnotes obscuring God's simple command to love your neighbor, it's probably because you feel pretty much the same way the Jewish lawyer felt about the Samaritans.

Why Didn't the Priest and the Levite Stop?

This poor man had been robbed and beaten half to death. Not only did the priest pass by without helping him; he also crossed the road and walked on the other side. A priest is someone who serves the people by making sacrifices to God on their behalf. This priest may have said to himself, *Well, he's not one of my parishioners; I shouldn't get involved. It's not my responsibility. He's not my neighbor.* New Testament scholar Joachim Jeremias writes, "It must be supposed that the priest and the Levite regarded the unconscious man as dead, and avoided contact with him [the wounded man] on Levitical grounds."[2] In either case, the priest's action conveyed an attitude of indifference, not one of ceremonial sensitivity.

A Levite was a servant to the priests. The Levites did all the manual labor, while the priests did the spiritual work regarding temple worship. The Levite, who would have been mentored by a priest, walked by, saw the same beaten, half-dead man, and never helped him. Though a man may have a religious affiliation, that does not mean he's going to be exemplary in terms of his attitude toward those who have been hurt by society. The Levite's behavior confirms my point.

The lawyer had cited the Law of Moses, which read:

> [17] "*'You shall not hate your fellow countryman in your heart;*
> *you may surely reprove your neighbor, but shall not incur*

*sin because of him. ¹⁸You shall not take vengeance, nor bear
any grudge against the sons of your people, but you shall
love your neighbor as yourself; I am the LORD.'"*

(Lev. 19:17–18 NAS)

Theologian Norval Geldenhuys writes in *The New London Commentary on the New Testament*, "All available data indicate that the Jewish religious leaders regarded *only* their own fellow-countrymen as their neighbors. According to the *Halakhah*, an Israelite's neighbor is any member of his nation but not one who is not an Israelite."[3] The parable of the Good Samaritan intentionally did not mention the wounded man's race or religious affiliation. Jesus' purpose was to get His audience to think through the primary issues of love, compassion, and humanitarian concern, rather than having them focus on nonessentials.

What the lawyer seemed to be asking Jesus, was *Does the command to love your neighbor as yourself extend to other races or even to those who are not considered to be God's covenant people?* What Jesus said to the lawyer through the parable could perhaps be summarized like this: *Love other people—rich people, poor people, victimized people, and even Samaritans—as yourself. That is, love them as if they were just like you. Do not segregate your love.*

The Man on the Way to Jericho Did Not Victimize Himself.

The wounds of the man traveling on the Jerusalem-to-Jericho road were not self-inflicted. This is a simple but important observation. How many times have you seen people who were the victims of crimes or who wound up out of a job and homeless? When you've seen or heard of such a situation, how often have you thought to yourself:

Who Is My Neighbor?

He probably got into that situation by his own doing.

She is probably lazy; that's why she's homeless.

Why didn't they take more initiative to do something with their lives?

They were crime victims because they chose to associate with the wrong group of people.

Everyone makes his or her share of good and bad choices in life. It's also true that a person's social and economic environment greatly increases or decreases his or her margin of error. A kid from the worst situation can indeed grow up to be a great success and fulfill all of his dreams—that is, if the kid makes *few* mistakes. He must also possess extraordinary drive, vision, diligence, resilience, self-control, and intelligence. Even with all this in place, success may only come with significant help from a gracious benefactor. On the other hand, kids in more advantageous situations have a high probability of success, even with *many* bad choices and less effort.

It's true that most kids fall somewhere in between the two extremes. The point is that the person panhandling on the street corner, the one who works for minimum wage, and the C.E.O. of a corporation have all made both good and bad choices. But there are many uncontrollable factors that have brought each person to where he is. People don't choose to become victims. They are usually caught up in a current that is simply too powerful to overcome.

Perhaps the priest and the Levite excused themselves because they considered that this man was somehow responsible for his situation. That is a very convenient perspective to take when it comes to other people and their problems. But the mandate of the kingdom of God is to show mercy without any attempt to assess blame. Don Stephens, president of Mercy Ships, explains in his book *Mandate for Mercy* the three approaches to mercy taken by the major world religions. In the *fatalistic worldview*, things are viewed as being the way they are because that's the way they were meant to be. If a people-group is oppressed, it's because it is their fate. That is precisely how the devastation in Bangladesh is viewed by many Hindus. In the *karmic worldview*, each individual is thought to be in a state of cosmic flux, moving up or down life's ladder through endless reincarnations. A person's place in life is based on his karma (i.e., what he has done in his past lives). It is only in the *Judeo-Christian worldview* that the individual is considered to be important to God simply because of who he is, not because of what he has done, good or bad. Don Stephens writes:

> In this respect, Christianity is unique. It is the only religion that has mercy coupled with action as one of its foundation stones. And the story of the Good Samaritan illustrates what should happen when Christians are confronted with the suffering and needs of others.[4]

Assuming that individuals or groups are responsible for their own victimization is usually an excuse to sidestep the mandates of the kingdom of God. Consequently, those who hold this worldview are able to simply pass by on the other side of the road, undisturbed by what they see.

Why Did the Good Samaritan Stop to Help?

Though I may not have victimized people, I still have a responsibility to heal them. A typical white person might think to himself, *I*

114

never hurt any black people. My great-grandfather came here from Europe three generations ago and was a soldier in the Union army, risking his life to emancipate the slaves! My grandfather was a good man, and my father never hurt anyone. I can't understand why African-americans feel so angry. Slavery was done away with over a hundred years ago. And we have had equal opportunity and affirmative action programs for decades. Why are they mad at me? I haven't done anything to hurt a black person. I wish they would just get over it.

It may be true that you bear no direct responsibility for these injustices against African-Americans. But that does not excuse you from empathizing with the hurts of the people in your community, especially when they are your brothers and sisters in Christ. Though I may not understand the sentiments of Native Americans who object to the mascots of various sports teams, I must nonetheless love my Native American brothers.

Though I may not intellectually or logically understand the sentiments of the Italian, Brazilian, or German communities, if they are incensed about something and we live together in the community of faith, I still have a moral obligation to be a part of the solution to their problem. Because of my love for them, I must accommodate their feelings. I am required to listen, to dialogue, and to see from their perspective. Because we live together in one community, I must ask, "What are some of the things you're going through? Are there things I do that offend you because I'm somehow different from you? What can I do to help you feel reconciled?"

Though we may think, feel, and act very differently, I want to be sensitive to what you feel because you are my brother or sister in Christ. Though I may not understand, and though I may even disagree, I won't just disregard your feelings and go on with business as usual. I will learn to be accommodating for the sake of Christ.

The interesting thing about being accommodating and empathetic is that it requires the assistance of the person in need of empathy. My wife has had to teach me how to understand and relate to her in different ways. If my pride or dogmatic views are preeminent, I may falsely conclude that I am meeting her needs, when all along I have been insensitive and ignorant of them. We can only begin to meet each other's marital needs when we engage in heartfelt dialogue. Similarly, relationships only achieve mutual respect and healthy displays of love through honest, open discussions. Achieving racial harmony requires the same things.

As I mentioned earlier, Jesus never discussed the ethnic origin of the man who was hurt. A robbery victim is a victim, regardless of his nationality. The reason the Samaritan stopped was that he felt compassion and empathy for the man. The Samaritan knew what it was like to be hated and rejected because of racial prejudice; it's not much different from being beaten up and robbed. Identifying with the sufferings of others connects you with them. There is a bond of commonality. I'm sure that others who passed by felt sorry for the man on some level. But they didn't personally identify with him in the ditch, nor they consider how he must have felt. Had the priest and the Levite allowed themselves to experience that kind of empathy, they could not have remained so detached from the man's situation. This is precisely what Jesus was getting at in the parable of the Good Samaritan. By narrowly defining who qualified as his brother, the lawyer had detached himself from the obligation to show love and mercy, except to those of his preference.

Religious people like this lawyer and the Pharisees were theological hair-splitters, and there are a lot of Christians like them today. These people are intent on being right and pointing out the inaccurate beliefs of everyone else. I cannot help but think that if we were equally intent on fulfilling the mandate to love our neighbors, the Holy Spirit would move in our midst much more freely. Sometimes it's better to be kind than to be right.

Love is Not a Project.

The lawyer posed the question to Jesus: "Teacher, what shall I do to inherit eternal life?" In the dialogue that followed, it became clear that the lawyer was trying to understand love in terms of a precise legal definition and to pinpoint the minimum requirement for obtaining eternal life. But when you try to love out of obligation, it's no longer a pure love. I call it "missionary love" or "project love."

Missionary love comes from a person who says to himself, *Well, God called me to these people, and it's obvious that they really need me. God has told me to love them, so I do.* Personally, I wouldn't enjoy or easily receive that type of love because it would cause me to feel like a project. After he'd completed his task and fulfilled his obligation to love me, there would be another notch in his belt and he'd be gone. Like the lawyer, he'd think of loving his neighbor as an unavoidable chore.

Large segments of the body of Christ have been guilty of doing just this. They can go to Africa and love people, but they can't go to Newark, New Jersey; South-Central Los Angeles; or a Native American reservation and love people. Some people share the gospel with others simply because they feel guilty when they don't and better about themselves when they do! It has little to do with love for other people. It's just a project.

STRAIGHTFORWARD LOVE, PURE AND SIMPLE

Prejudice exists in people of all races. Those who have been the victims of prejudice are very often prejudiced themselves. Christians from all races who say that the Lord has saved them sometimes compartmentalize their lives. There are dark, dirty closets that have yet to be cleaned. All of this is covered up by phony religious jargon. These believers say that they love God and all men, but their actions speak otherwise.

Because we are members of the same family under God, our Father, we need to be honest with each other. If you love me, you'll talk to me straight. Though it may hurt, reconciliation begins when we truthfully speak to one another in love. That's the only way to get beyond superficial reconciliation—the kind that merely puts a bandage on the problem. When you personally commit yourself to reconciliation, people will want to listen to you because they'll realize that your statements are made out of genuine love.

Much is said about the gifts and power of God being the evidence of whether a person has been filled with the Holy Spirit, and so they are. However, an equally profound manifestation of the outpouring of the Spirit on the day of Pentecost was the degree to which all those having received the Spirit were bound together in unity. Indeed, they had "all things in common." Whenever there is revival or an outpouring of the Spirit, people are drawn closer together—often closer than they have ever been to any group in their lives. A true manifestation of the Holy Spirit is that people are "in one accord."

The internal transforming power of Jesus Christ is evidenced by: 1) a commitment to righteousness; and, 2) the attitudes and actions we display toward our fellow man. As I said before, God's truth is simple and straightforward. The apostle John put it this way: *"By this the children of God and the children of the devil are obvious: anyone who does not practice righteousness is not of God, nor the one who does not love his brother. For this is the message which you have heard from the beginning, that we should love one another"* (1 John 3:10–11). Because we are new creatures in Christ, we can learn to love the Archie Bunkers and the George Jeffersons (bigots portrayed in American television comedies) of the world, even if they don't love us. How much easier, then, should it be to truly love our brother and sisters in Christ who happen to be of a different race?

Because we are all in the same community of faith and have now become one man in Christ, we must be reconciled to each other. Let's learn to love each other. Let's learn to become sensitive to one another. Though we may have visible external differences, because Christ is in me, my behavior toward you should model what the kingdom of God is like. Let's learn to foster this model so that when the world sees the church, they see a prototype of what true community is supposed to be like.

—— *Chapter 8* ——

THE INITIATIVE OF RECONCILIATION

R*econciliation* has become a buzzword in Christian circles today. But all too often the people using the word have not grasped its full essence, or their understanding of the word is not consistent with the biblical meaning. Consequently, the reconciliation they envision and experience falls far short of the God-initiated experience described in the Bible.

Western culture had its roots and worldview in the Bible. As a whole, people today (Christians included) are less familiar with Christian theology and the precise meanings of theological terms than at any other time since the Protestant Reformation. Nevertheless, because of our Christian heritage, biblical and theological words make up a large part of our modern vocabulary. Often we accept commonly used meanings for words such as *restoration, restitution,* and *reconciliation* rather than learning their true meanings. To understand and experience reconciliation as God has designed it, we need to first clarify exactly what reconciliation means from a biblical perspective.

The term *reconciliation* is found eight times in the Bible—five times in the Old Testament and three in the New Testament. Its verb form, *to reconcile*, is found five times in Scripture—three in the Old Testament and two in the New Testament. Salvation involves not only the removal of guilt, but also the development of a personal relationship with God. The word *reconciliation* is used often as a synonym for salvation. Paul wrote, *"We beg you on behalf of Christ, be reconciled to God"* (2 Cor. 5:20b NAS). In other words, Paul was saying, "We beg you to be saved."

Only in Judaism and Christianity is there the promise of a personal relationship with the omnipotent God. Consequently, *reconciliation with God* as a theological concept is found only in the Judeo-Christian tradition. New Testament scholar Herman Ridderbos writes, "This is clearly evident from the context of the reconciliation pronouncements in 2 Corinthians 5. Reconciliation constitutes the foundation of the new creation, of the fact that the old has passed away, that the new has come (2 Cor. 5:17, 18), of the 'now' of the day of salvation and of the acceptable time."[1]

As you know, the gospel message of Jesus—His death, burial, and resurrection—captures the clearest picture of eternal salvation and therefore of reconciliation as well. If we examine the definition, etymology, and usage of these terms in the New Testament era, we can develop a contemporary model of restoring relationships that is consistent with the highest and most perfect form of reconciliation—that of God reconciling mankind to Himself through Christ.

The biblical meaning of *reconciliation* is so important that Paul defines the gospel of the kingdom with the phrase *"the word of reconciliation"* (2 Cor. 5:19 NAS). In Romans 5:9–10 (NAS), *"justified by His blood"* parallels the phrase *"reconciled to God through the death of His Son."* In 2 Corinthians 3:9 and 5:18 (NAS), the phrases *"ministry of righteousness"* and *"ministry of reconciliation"* are interchangeable.

Though there is parallel usage of these terms, a technical difference still must be noted. Ridderbos and other New Testament scholars add that "to justify" is a religious-forensic (i.e., legal) concept, whereas "reconciliation," in a general sense, has a social flavor due to its origin in the social-societal sphere.[2]

THE MEANING OF SOCIETAL RECONCILIATION

The word *reconciliation* is translated from the New Testament Greek word *katallasso*, which means "to change mutually." It is the compound of two words, *kata* ("pertaining to; concerning") and *allasso* ("to make different; to change"). Prior to its acceptance into the Christian vernacular, the word *reconciliation* was used by the Greeks to refer to the exchange of coins.[3] It is still used today as an accounting term, as in "The ledger must be reconciled."

In addition to its use in the banking and accounting spheres, reconciliation has a social dimension. Paul instructs us regarding how we ought to correct marital disputes, saying, *"To the married I give this command (not I, but the Lord): A wife must not separate from her husband. But if she does, she must remain unmarried or else be reconciled to her husband. And a husband must not divorce his wife"* (1 Cor. 7:10–11). The usual counsel for severely strained marriages is temporary separation. This separation must be the last option, since communication typically breaks down once people move away from one another. Paul gives the instruction "be reconciled" to the separated party. Thus, reconciliation has a social connotation. A strained marriage can only improve once friendship is resumed. Reconciliation incorporates friendship, communication, harmony, and togetherness in its biblical usage and meaning.

A couple formerly separated due to the unhealthy state of their marriage cannot achieve this depth of reconciliation unless the period of estrangement results in a rebuilding program for their marriage. The problems that led to the separation must be resolved before a healthy

123

reunion can take place. In addition, the way in which solutions were reached prior to the separation was obviously wrong. Thus, reconciliation involves a rebuilding, remaking, and restoring stage. Consequently, when the Holy Spirit chose to use this word throughout the New Testament to describe the work of Christ on the cross, He was conveying the idea of restoring the old materials of a gutted building with new, contemporary furnishings. A building that was formerly unusable is now rendered usable. Reconciled marriages go through the same restorative process.

This process of restoration is exactly what God did with man. He made possible the opportunity for us to *"lay aside the old self, which is being corrupted in accordance with the lusts of deceit...and put on the new self, which in the likeness of God has been created in righteousness and holiness of the truth"* (Eph. 4:22–24 NAS). The lifestyle of sin, which occupied our earthly body, was gutted and replaced by new furnishings—righteousness and holiness. Reconciliation is the act of both reconciling an estranged relationship and restoring it to its original purpose and former glory.

RECONCILIATION AS AN ACT OF GOD

The most complete biblical statement of reconciliation is contained in Paul's second letter to the Corinthians:

> [17]*Therefore if any man is in Christ, he is a new creature; the old things passed away; behold, new things have come.* [18]*Now all these things are from God, who reconciled us to Himself through Christ, and gave us the ministry of reconciliation, namely,* [19]*that God was in Christ reconciling the world to Himself, not counting their trespasses against them,*

and He has committed to us the word of reconciliation.
[20]Therefore, we are ambassadors for Christ, as though God
were entreating through us; we beg you on behalf of Christ,
be reconciled to God. [21]He made Him who knew no sin to
be sin on our behalf, that we might become the righteous-
ness of God in Him. (2 Cor. 5:17–21 NAS)

When the historical meaning of reconciliation is applied to these portions of Scripture, we gain a new appreciation for God's gracious action toward man in his alienated and sinful state. Sin separates humanity from God. God is a perfect, holy Judge, as well as a perfectly loving Father. The separation is legal, judicial, and relational. With regard to man's legal separation from God, Jesus, through His atoning death, removed sin and thereby legally justified us before God. Though our sin and guilt never quenched God's love for us, it prevented us from receiving the gift of the Holy Spirit, who was given to dwell in our hearts. Having been legally reconciled to the standard of God's perfect justice by the blood of Christ, we can now be restored to a personal relationship with God by the indwelling presence of the Holy Spirit.

The passage cited above (2 Cor. 5:17–21) clearly indicates that it was God's initiative to reconcile man to Himself. Cecil B. Murphey writes, "Reconciliation is God's own completed act that takes place before human actions such as confession, repentance and restitution."[4]

Note that there was no need for God to be reconciled to man. Many who quote Bible verses about forgiveness and reconciliation would never think of initiating reconciliation when the other person is completely at fault. But the act of reconciliation that was initiated by God was a response to man's need to be reconciled to Him. Philip E. Hughes writes, "It is [God] who reconciles us, and it is to Himself that He reconciles us. Reconciliation proceeds from God and returns to God."[5]

All that is truly good, worthy, and morally right is so because it's a reflection of the nature of God. In short, lying is wrong because God does not lie. Moreover, He *cannot* lie because in His unchangeable nature, He is a God of truth. Should we then initiate reconciliation with those who have sinned against us? Indeed, it is the right thing to do because this is precisely what God did for us in Christ.

The passage from 2 Corinthians also reveals what God had in mind as the purpose and continuing result of reconciliation. God was able to restore the breach in fellowship with man through the means of reconciliation. Alienation, sin, and man's darkened state were not powerful enough to overcome the force of Christ's ministry of reconciliation. The long estrangement between man and God did not exhaust the power of God to restore the relationship. In other words, reconciliation forms a bridge between God and man across the great divide that sin created. That bridge of reconciliation is the pathway to peace and personal relationship with God.

Although the Scriptures we've analyzed focus on vertical reconciliation (i.e., man being restored to a right relationship with God), these principles readily apply to horizontal reconciliation—divided individuals, groups, races, and nations being restored to a right relationship with each other.

STEPS TOWARD RECONCILIATION

Second Corinthians 5:17–21 contains four steps to achieving reconciliation. God pursued man in order to show him his need for restoration, and then He provided the means of restoration. Reconciliation, which leads to restoration, is not something attained by do-gooders who haphazardly stumbled upon this fortunate experience. It was a calculated act of God. The greatest divide ever created was the gulf formed between sinful man and a holy God. If man, through Jesus Christ, was able to achieve the greatest of all restorations, think how much more successful we can be when we apply the same principles to the lesser problem of racism!

Since we are covenant sons and daughters of God (John 1:12), we have a legal responsibility to model the behavior of our heavenly Father. Jesus said, *"For whatever the Father does, these things the Son also does in like manner"* (John 5:19 NAS). We are to put on the character and attributes of God in order to achieve racial reconciliation. If we put on love, *"for God is love"* (1 John 4:8 NAS), we will be able to model diversity.

God, in His infinite wisdom, humbled Himself and put on the attire of human flesh in order to carry out His strategic plan of reconciling the unsympathetic race of humanity. Therefore, Peter admonishes us as well to *"clothe [ourselves] with humility toward one another, because, 'God opposes the proud but gives grace to the humble'"* (1 Pet. 5:5).

The following four principles are not simply theological points to be hashed over by intellectuals. They must be viewed in much the same way as articles of clothing; they must be "put on" in order for the goal of racial reconciliation to be met. God employed these steps to restore fallen man to Himself. We can duplicate them to form bonds of racial unity with those from whom we're presently alienated due to racism or cultural ignorance. These biblical principles can be applied to modern-day situations and circumstances. However, the reconciliation of racial wars, like any solution to a major societal problem, requires both a genuine commitment to and an understanding of the biblical process.

Step #1: Recognizing the Problem

We live in a fallen world, with problems all around us. This fact is accentuated in the information age, in which the accumulated bad news of the entire globe is served up each evening on the nightly news. Eventually, we become desensitized to the problems ailing society.

Just imagine being born and raised in "beautiful downtown Sodom." Living amid the debauchery of that community would probably harden your heart toward moral unrighteousness. After a while, you'd begin to think that a lifestyle of sinfulness is normal. This is analogous to the problem of racism and the church. Prejudice, separation, and racial isolation have existed for so long that Bible-believing, Spirit-filled people are desensitized to them. They are the only responses we have known.

God noted man's separated state and decided to act unilaterally in order to solve the problem. In other words, He took the initiative. Christians must see that racial alienation is the result of the sins of prejudice and racism, both in the world and in the church. Experiencing the new birth should alter a person's value system, priorities, and outlook on life. A Christian who has been reconciled by the grace of God must respond to that merciful act by showing mercy and grace as a reconciler himself. Recipients of mercy should always be sensitive to others in need of mercy.

Jesus told the story of an unmerciful slave who had been forgiven an enormous debt because the king felt compassion on him. That slave, in turn, was unwilling to forgive a fellow slave a comparatively insignificant debt. The king heard of it, summoned the unmerciful slave, and said, *"You wicked slave, I forgave you all that debt because you entreated me. Should you not also have had mercy on your fellow slave, even as I had mercy on you?"* (Matt. 18:32–33 NAS). The king was moved with anger and had the slave placed in the debtors' prison until he paid back every cent. Jesus concluded the story by saying, *"So shall My heavenly Father also do to you, if each of you does not forgive his brother from your heart"* (Matt. 18:35 NAS).

The famous hymn "Amazing Grace" was written in the late 1700s by John Newton, a former slave ship captain who was overwhelmed by the mercy God had extended to him. However, Kenneth Osbeck writes, "For the next several years [Newton] continued as a slave ship captain, trying to justify his work by seeking to improve conditions as much as possible, even holding public worship services for his hardened crew of thirty each Sunday."[6] Newton eventually discontinued this unrighteous occupation because he recognized that it conflicted with his new faith in Christ. Indeed, man's natural tendency is to rationalize rather than recognize sin, lest he be called upon to do something about it.

Step #2: Judging the Problem

Recognizing the existence of a sin and then choosing to ignore it is unthinkable to a genuine child of God. The phrase "I'm waiting on the leading of the Lord" is commonly used as a spiritual escape mechanism. But the epistle of James tells us, *"Anyone, then, who knows the good he ought to do and doesn't do it, sins"* (James 4:17). How can Christians sit idly by while the bride of Christ (the church) is being ravaged by racism? This occurs when the church either refuses to recognize the problem or fails to discern the seriousness of the sin.

True judgment is being able to see things through God's eyes. Even Jesus said, *"I can do nothing on My own initiative. As I hear, I judge; and My judgment is just, because I do not seek My own will, but the will of Him who sent Me"* (John 5:30 NAS). The perspective of fallen man always minimizes sin. We say, "Yes, I know it is sin, but...." The words that follow, in one way or another, convey that the sin is not grievous enough to require any action. It's what you might call "recognition without conviction." The ministry of the Holy Spirit, according to Jesus, is to *"convict the world of guilt in regard to sin and righteousness and judgment"* (John 16:8). In other words, the Holy Spirit motivates people through the steps of recognition (sin), realization (judgment), and action (righteousness).

Reconciliation cannot take place in or out of the church until we face the sins of injustice in our past. The wrongs committed by our white forefathers against our Native American ancestors cannot go unnoticed by the church. Indeed, in the process of judging, many excuse themselves because they were not personally responsible for slavery or other acts of racial injustice. But the question arises: Can the judgment of God and responsibility for past injustices transcend generations? Such an instance is recorded in 2 Samuel.

> *Now there was a famine in the days of David for three years, year after year; and David sought the presence of the LORD. And the LORD said, "It is for Saul and his bloody house, because he put the Gibeonites to death."* (2 Sam. 21:1 NAS)

The Gibeonites were the Canaanite inhabitants of the city of Gibeon. When Joshua had invaded the land of Canaan, a delegation of Gibeonites had come to him with stale bread and dressed in ragged clothes (Josh. 9:4–5). Pretending they were from a distant country, they persuaded Joshua, who did not seek the Lord in the matter, to make a treaty with them. Even though the Gibeonites were deceivers, God demanded that Joshua keep his word.

Many years later, Saul's patriotic zeal drove him to kill some of the Gibeonites who were dwelling in Israel. Then, during the reign of David—who had had nothing to do with killing the Gibeonites—the judgment of God came upon Israel in the form of a famine. The stated reason for this was that Saul had not abided by a long-standing foreign policy agreement.

Step #3: Taking the Initiative

Our omnipotent God initiated the process of reconciliation by breaking the communication barrier in order to connect with mankind. Philippians 2 contains a creed that dates back to the earliest days of the Christian church:

> *⁵Have this attitude in yourselves which was also in Christ Jesus, ⁶who, although He existed in the form of God, did not regard equality with God a thing to be grasped, ⁷but emptied Himself, taking the form of a bond-servant, and being made in the likeness of men. ⁸And being found in appearance as a man, He humbled Himself by becoming obedient to the point of death, even death on a cross.*
>
> (Phil. 2:5–8 NAS)

This act of reconciliation displayed God's recognition, His judgment, and His initiative, which bridged the gap caused by sin and solved the problem of man's alienation. If the almighty God can humble Himself and take the introductory steps toward restoration, why do we hesitate in taking the first steps to bring healing? Isn't it ironic that God, who is perfect in all He does, is willing to humble Himself, while man, who is himself the recipient of amazing grace and forgiveness, refuses to do so?

Have you ever seen two little children get upset over who needs to apologize to whom? One child cries, "He hit me first. He should say 'I'm sorry.'" The second child responds, "She made me hit her. She should apologize."

Taking the first step toward a "peace talk" is always difficult. Not only do you have to get over asking, *Why should I take the first step?* You also have to deal with the pressures placed on you by those of your own race.

It takes a lot of courage to walk across a social divide. That kind of courage and humility was demonstrated by Egyptian president Anwar el-Sadat in November of 1977, when he flew to Jerusalem for talks with Menachem Begin, the prime minister of Israel. In doing so, he paved the way for peace between Egypt and Israel. Of course, he was greatly criticized by radical Arab factions that wanted nothing to do with reconciliation. In 1981 Sadat's critics assassinated him. But in taking steps toward peace, he proved himself to be the greatest of all the leaders in the region.

Jesus said, *"If therefore you are presenting your offering at the altar, and there remember that your brother has something against you, leave your offering there before the altar, and go your way; first be reconciled to your brother, and then come and present your offering"* (Matt. 5:23–24 NAS). The edict to go does not necessarily suggest who is at fault. If anything, it implies that the one unjustly treated should go to his brother. The principle of the kingdom is that *"without any dispute the lesser is blessed by the greater"* (Heb. 7:7 NAS). A greater, more Christlike person has no problem reaching out to someone in a spirit of humility for the sake of building a relationship.

Step #4: The Problem is Reconciled

Husbands and wives often have very different opinions about whether or not a problem has been solved. In most cases, it's the husband who is satisfied with the reconciliation, while his wife feels that the problem has not been adequately addressed. It's the same way with racism. Each party has its own opinion as to what it takes to achieve genuine reconciliation and restoration. Anything that falls short of the biblical standard of reconciliation fails to solve the problem completely. It's not unlike cutting down weeds in the garden. If they're not completely uprooted, they will very soon return.

Individuals who serve as catalysts of reconciliation must be mindful of the psychological and relational dynamics of unity. Open dialogue, accompanied by sincere vulnerability on both sides, must be encouraged. Those involved in facilitating such an exchange of ideas should seek to open a discussion of past hurts, misconceptions, and biases on the way to finding workable solutions to problems.

Always remember that steps toward reconciliation take time. As representatives from different races start down the road of reconciliation, they have to be careful to avoid the many land mines left from years of racial tension. When one person begins to share feelings of bitterness and prejudice that are laced with negative stereotypes, this places a great demand on the other party's humility, patience, and commitment to the goal of reconciliation. If not skillfully handled, these expressions can pose a serious threat to the goal. You must remember the prize in order to stay focused on finding pragmatic solutions. The ability to overlook offenses is exemplified in the plan of redemption: *"God was in Christ reconciling the world to Himself, not counting [taking an inventory of] their trespasses against them"* (2 Cor. 5:19 NAS). When offenses are reconciled and relationships are restored, taking an inventory of sins is no longer an issue.

Practicing the Four Steps

The experience of the Jamaican gentleman I referred to in chapter 5 is noteworthy to me, seeing that he was able to move from the point of prejudice to that of an authentic reconciler. The four steps toward reconciliation were employed with the assistance of the Holy Spirit. Twenty years after the firebombing of his home, John is now able to have meaningful and open friendships with white people.

Following his conversion to Christ, John *recognized* that the firebombing incident had alienated him from whites. This alienation led to his feeling awkward around all other races when he had to interact in a personal, nonbusiness setting. So, he *judged* the situation. He discovered that hatred, prejudice, and bigotry had weighed him down, causing him to live beneath the biblical standard of unity. Following a time of deep introspection and personal confrontation, he took the *initiative* to love his enemies, to forgive them of their trespasses against his family, and to bridge the social divide. Finally, after being relationally reconciled to the white race, he was able to establish true friendships with white people.

Chapter 9

CREATING AN EXPRESSION OF KINGDOM DIVERSITY

When I was growing up, my mother would always tell me, "David, if you create the right environment, you can grow practically anything you want." Years later, when I was married and we had children, Mom again rehearsed those words to me. This time she was using the cliché to help me realize that I could teach my children to love reading and education by creating the right academic climate in my home. After several years of nurturing this special environment within my home, I can say, "Praise God! Mom was right again."

The other day, I was eavesdropping on my five-year-old's conversation with one of her playmates, and I overheard her correcting the other little girl's grammar. I chuckled to myself because this cute scene confirmed what can happen when the church creates the right dynamics for the acceptance of various ethnic groups.

During the formative years of Christ Church, I knew that the vision of diversity had to be firmly fixed in the hearts of the congregation. This required a scholarly and practical treatise on the causes and problems of racial disunity. We also needed to present the joys of unity in ways that would ensure adoption of the message. At times I used strong, direct preaching to break up the hard ground of the members' hearts. At other times I used humor to show how God could use people like us to model diversity in an age of division.

We were committed to moving ahead with the vision of building a cross-cultural, multiracial congregation. It was exciting to announce to all our vision, our hopes, and even our fears. We knew it was God's desire, so we labored tirelessly, at times with many questions. Today, we're still at the grindstone, working to make a difference in the world. The effort to become world-class Christians is a noble one, and it requires a real commitment.

Every now and then I come across leaders who have a hard time distinguishing between their vision for an organization and its present reality. They are so passionate about where they want to go and what they want to happen that they can see it clearly, as if it already exists. I once heard of a pastor who refused to allow anyone on his ministry team to "quench his vision" by bringing up anything negative in staff meetings. Everyone was to have only a "good report." Of course, *he* always thought everything was going great. But working through problems was a maddening process for the staff. Unless a visionary leader has a faithful and trusted administrative team standing with him, the impassioned leader may make decisions, promises, and commitments based on a reality that exists only in his own mind.

Many visionary leaders also have a problem with patience. By always looking ahead, focusing on the vision of what is to be, they often overlook all the practical things that must be done in order for the organization to arrive at its destination. It takes time and steady plodding to accomplish significant things. Good leaders are able to remain focused and passionate about their vision, but at the same time, they understand the reality of process.

I had the opportunity of leading a fellow engineering student to Christ while I was in graduate school. I took my next role of discipling him rather seriously. I used to visit him in his dorm twice a week to answer his questions and fellowship with him. I had only accepted Christ a year earlier. Now, here I was trying to disciple someone when I needed to be discipled myself. On one of these visits, I walked into my friend's dorm room to find him sitting by the open window with only a pair of shorts on. It was January, and the outside temperature was no warmer than fifteen degrees above zero. It was cold—freezing cold. I asked him why he was sitting by the open window practically naked. I'll never forget his youthful reply: "I'm trying to crucify my flesh so that I can serve God more effectively."

I blurted out such a loud laugh that the guys down the hall could hear me. But the look on my friend's face showed that my laughter was hurtful to him. He was serious about his desire to crucify his flesh. After he closed the window and got dressed, I immediately began telling him about the process of sanctification. I'm sure I didn't fully understand this doctrine myself back then. But I was sure that my friend's vision to be pure before the Lord could not be fully attained in one evening.

My friend was a lot like Moses, who got really fired up about being the deliverer of God's chosen people. Moses even killed an Egyptian in an attempt to help one of the Hebrew slaves. As a result, he was stripped of his power and privilege, thrown out of Pharaoh's household, and exiled in the wilderness. Not only that! The Hebrews whom he was attempting to help didn't even appreciate what he was trying to do. Moses did indeed become a great deliver. But it was not by his strength and zeal. God took Moses through a process to equip him to be a God-empowered, God-inspired leader who was right on schedule with the divine timetable.

For those of us who feel called to be reconcilers and kingdom builders, there's a process too. Here are a few steps to keep in mind.

1. Be Clear About Your Calling.

Whenever a person swims against the stream or goes against conventional wisdom and practice, there's going to be a backlash. Many members of Christ Church have had to bear criticism from people of their own race or ethnic group. Other African-Americans question our African-American members: *"What are you doing over there with those white people?"* To many of their critics, cross-cultural relationships are an either-or proposition. To them, associating with whites means rejecting their own race. Their friends have also called some African-americans at Christ Church "oreos." Calling someone an "oreo" is like saying that they are black on the outside and white on the inside, like an Oreo cookie.

I also realize that every white person in my church has paid a price to be there. The sacrifice whites make is different from and often greater than that of most minorities in America. People who live as minorities have had the everyday experience of fitting in with another culture. Members of the majority group can and often do spend their entire lives never having been in a situation in which they, by necessity, had to adjust to another culture. When an individual from a majority group intentionally takes that kind of step, it's not only more difficult, but also more unconventional. Consequently, more people notice, and line up to register their disapproval. I've said from the pulpit on several occasions, "Every nonminority person sitting in this church has made a sacrificial commitment to be here with the rest of you this morning. You need to understand that, and you need to know what it means to be accommodating to them."

Most people who have been around for a while and who've had an opportunity to build some cross-cultural relationships understand this. But for other minorities at Christ Church, it comes as a real surprise. It has never occurred to them that other ethnic groups experience some of the same feelings of rejection, needing to be accepted, and insecurity that they have experienced. Once they realize this, they have great empathy.

On the other hand, members of predominately white congregations are even less likely to understand what some minorities go through in order to come to their church. They have had no experience as minorities and have a hard time identifying with their situation, even after it's pointed out.

The apostle Peter wrote, *"Therefore, brethren, be all the more diligent to make certain about His calling and choosing you"* (2 Pet. 1:10 NAS). In this passage, the apostle was exhorting his readers to diligence, perseverance, and brotherly kindness. The calling Peter referred to was a general call to be a part of God's kingdom. Since I believe that inclusion and diversity are characteristics of the kingdom of God, I also believe that every follower of Jesus Christ will to some degree be called to personally incorporate and model those principles. Beyond that, there are many ministers and laymen who are called to lead the way in demonstrating this characteristic of the kingdom to a society that so badly needs to see it.

If a long-term commitment to what God has called you to do is not settled in your heart and mind, you can be easily swayed by circumstances. Every setback and opposing force will cause you to reconsider your calling and purpose. Those people who step forward to lead the way need to spend time before the Lord and "make certain about His calling and choosing."

That doesn't mean that you're so sure of God's calling that you never doubt. It does mean that you sense God's initiative. You are not doing something out of your own initiative to please God, to please man, or just to be different. In other words, you are not trying to talk God into blessing what you want to do for Him. You sense that this is what *He's* doing, and that He's saying, "Follow Me."

I've personally found that if your mission is to build a model of diversity—the kingdom on earth as it is in heaven—then God will be with you to supply what you need to be successful. But I've also learned that success doesn't come without difficulties. Consequently, a clear commitment to your mission must first be established.

2. Individual Models Come First.

Modeling the kingdom personally must take place before modeling the kingdom corporately. Diversity among the senior leader's personal relationships must first be established. Be careful of your intentions. Create and foster real, not token or "project" relationships. By "project" relationships, I mean cross-cultural relationships with an ulterior motive. True friendship exists for its own sake. Trust me: You'll never be successful trying to befriend people of other races and cultures with a hidden agenda. They've almost certainly seen it before, and they are probably a lot more alert to your motives than you realize. In fact, most cross-cultural relationships take time because you have to prove there's no hook, no sales pitch, and no conditions.

When you try to model diversity, you need to understand that biases may have been fused into your cultural perspective, many of which you're not even aware. The language of some individuals is so monolithic that it insults people. It's like bad breath; you're the last one to know you have it. Many whites have grown up in an environment where there was an underlying, if not overt, assumption of racial superiority. Depending on the extent to which remnants of these ideas linger in a person's spirit, minorities and ethnic groups will pick up on them. This attitude of superiority will be communicated verbally and nonverbally, in ways of which the person is completely unaware.

A white missionary to an African nation made this comment to me: "In the country where I serve, when native Africans see a white man walking toward them, they sometimes make a comment which could be translated, 'He is a proud and prejudiced man.'" The missionary had asked the native Africans how they could know that, having never met the man. The tribesmen had said, "We can tell by the way he walks." The missionary discovered that oppressed people have a sixth sense by which they can identify the spirit of an oppressor or someone out to take advantage of them.

You can't build a successful corporate model unless you've worked through such dynamics and established an individual model. Building one-on-one multicultural relationships will cause you to find out some interesting things about yourself. You may discover prejudicial attitudes you never knew you had. That's when the Holy Spirit starts dealing with your heart, exposing attitudes that have come out of the unsanctified areas of your life. When you see this happening, you can be sure that you're on the road to becoming an authentic reconciler, rather than someone who merely expounds social theories.

The proverb says, *"As iron sharpens iron, so one man sharpens another"* (Prov. 27:17). God uses close relationships to smooth our rough edges. Some of the most practical and important lessons I have learned about cross-cultural relationships have come not from the many books I've read on the subject, but from close friends of other races who took me aside and said, "Listen, David, I've got to tell you something...."

We all have blind spots—things that others can see in us that we don't see. Multicultural relationships become mirrors, enabling us to see ourselves as others see us. Paul exhorted the Ephesians, *"Speaking the truth in love, we are to grow up in all aspects into Him"* (Eph. 4:15 NAS). God uses friends who love us enough to speak the truth to us as a means of dealing with "all aspects" of our lives, even our blind spots.

Leaders are by nature very self-confident. However, no one should set out to bridge cultural gaps by thinking he knows it all. Those who forge ahead with a handful of easy answers will have a rude awakening and realize they don't understand as much as they thought they did. You don't want to be like the proverbial bull in a china shop. You must move ahead as a learner and a servant.

I've seen people get so inspired with the vision of reconciliation and kingdom diversity that they simply fell over themselves trying to be accommodating. They've reminded me of a scene from a television comedy in which a white person tried to talk and act like "a brother from the hood." What made the scene comical was that the white guy seemed so phony. He was trying hard—maybe a little too hard.

I can work on my vocabulary and adjust certain areas in my life, but I'm still going to stick out as being culturally different. I can't change who God made me to be, nor should I. God made me who I am, and if I try to change that, I'll miss the purpose He has for me. God's plan is not that we lose our individuality or our cultural identity, but that all of us become bound together by something greater than the things that divide those who are outside the kingdom.

At first glance, it may be difficult to understand the fine line between cultural identity and cultural offensiveness. No doubt, some people will be offended by your identity, and there is simply nothing you can do about that. Modeling diversity on an individual level by building personal relationships with people of other races enables us to learn to discern between our God-given identities and the things we do that are offensive. It is only in personal relationships with covenant brothers that you're going to figure this out.

3. Learn How to Accommodate Others.

If my commitment to the kingdom is sincere, I will go beyond "diversity talk" and take practical steps in order to make people feel comfortable in my midst. In other words, I will plan for others to be with me and my church family. When I "set the table" in a way that is sensitive to other people, it not only makes *them* feel welcome; it also teaches those already sitting at the table that they too need to be accommodating.

Music is one of the most important areas of multicultural expression in the kingdom of God. In building a multicultural congregation, the way you approach music and worship will either make it or break it. At Christ Church, we sing hymns, gospel songs, contemporary music, jazz—even Beethoven is appreciated. It all blends together to create a style that is neither black, white, nor anything else.

Multicultural worship is more than singing one black song, then one white song, then one Hispanic song, then one Caribbean song, and so on. The key is in learning to appreciate the power of diversity. Since worship is such a vital part of appreciating diversity, the next chapter is dedicated solely to the topic. However, for the purpose of highlighting the need to be accommodating, allow me to use cross-cultural worship as an example.

The culture and heritage of the African-American community has given birth to worship that touches the emotions and gives full expression of the inner man to God. Its roots go back to American slavery. In those days, the only thing that slaves had of their own was their private gathering for worship. It is a well-established fact that spiritual life tends to flourish more under oppression and suffering than it does in a place of prosperity and free expression. Worldly temptations have always had more of a dulling effect on spirituality than persecution. Consequently, African-American worship is a passionate worship because it was born out of suffering and continued as such, long after slavery was officially abolished.

In the last twenty to thirty years, African-American worship has had a huge impact on how the body of Christ as a whole worships. People looking for a more expressive worship experience have borrowed heavily from this tradition. This is not to say that the traditional hymns of predominately white churches are not a valuable part of worship.

Most of the denominations in America, primarily Lutherans, Methodists, Baptists, and Presbyterians, came from Europe. Their heritage is based in Reformation theology. While African-American worship is influenced by the struggle for faith in the midst of suffering, European-American worship was birthed in a place where Christianity was popular. Religious conflicts in Europe were usually over theological interpretation and the ecclesiastical authority of various schools of thought. European Christianity, as a whole, was far more focused on an intellectual pursuit—a discussion of the fine points of theology. As a result, classical hymns from the sixteenth through the twentieth century have their own unique way of touching the human spirit. They convey a profound sense of the majesty and greatness of God. How much we need to incorporate each other's strengths!

Put simply, monolithic worship just doesn't push all the buttons. People *need* to worship in different ways. Worship should touch both the emotions and the intellect. It should get me to laugh. It should get me to weep. It should build my faith and break my heart. It should get me to celebrate. It should encourage me to be bold for the Lord. And it should cause me to contemplate the greatness of God. All these things are of equal importance.

Most black and white churches have already incorporated portions of each other's tradition. For many churches, becoming culturally friendly is simply a matter of recognizing: 1) the impact of different kinds of worship; 2) the origins of things they have already borrowed from each other; 3) the need to "just do it" some more; and, 4) the need to use their strengths to help other churches that may not have their level of expertise in this particular area.

Minority pastors face an entirely different set of challenges. For a long time, blacks didn't run the banks, the country clubs, the schools, and so forth. But they did have their own churches. The minority church has always been a refuge, where people could be themselves, without having to accommodate to the norms of another group. The pastor, more than any other minority individual, has never had to accommodate cultural diversity. Consequently, minority pastors are not very good at it. They too are challenged to be learners.

BIRTHING PASSION

With some personal experience modeling the diversity of the kingdom under your belt, you cannot help but begin to broadcast your ideas to others. This too requires patience, because it takes some time for people to change. I've seen people who've spent half their lives running from God before they got saved. These same people get frustrated and impatient with others who don't readily receive Christ the first time they hear the gospel.

As a pastor, I've learned that significant changes take place only when you lead by influence. You can't mandate that people think, perceive, or act the way you do. Good leaders have the ability to enroll people in their vision. Another way of putting it is that you enable people to "own the vision." Following along with what the church or the pastor believes is replaced by a personal commitment.

Church can be like a basketball game—a multicultural gathering without personal connections. Just because you're in a church that's racially and culturally diverse doesn't mean that you've dealt with prejudice. A person may enjoy the dynamics of that setting—the preaching, the drama, and the worship—but never have personalized it. He only *tolerates* the multicultural part.

There are a number of blacks in my congregation who enjoy my ministry but who are not multicultural, and I know it. They are still very monolithic. If I go to their birthday parties, all I can see is one ethnic group. They have not embraced the vision of the house, and after many years, their lives still haven't taken on diversity.

In order to birth passion and dedication in people, you have to communicate with them on both an intellectual and an emotional level. I began to preach at Christ Church about Christ-centeredness, kingdom-centeredness, and becoming global Christians. As an engineer, I was used to dealing with mathematical formulas. In that environment, once you prove your point mathematically, the matter is settled. I discovered, though, that it doesn't work that way with people. Though I could prove to someone that racial prejudice is wrong, I couldn't change people. Individuals with long-term commitments to prejudicial thinking don't want to be confused with the facts.

Emotions often hinder logic. What people believe has a lot to do with how they feel. So I began by asking some questions:

How would you feel if you went to church in a foreign country?

How would you feel about adopting a child of a different race?

Would you teach the child about her own culture, or only about yours?

What are some things you'd have to give up to be part of a multiracial church?

People began to realize not only what they had to give up, but also what they were holding on to. They began to ask themselves whether they were Christ-centered or culturally centered.

4. Reach Out to Minorities as Peers.

White congregations need to realize that minorities don't want a big brother, a teacher, or someone to look over their shoulders and tell them what to do. If that's what you're bringing to the relationship, you will probably never accomplish what God is looking for.

Many middle- and upper-class whites reach out to the inner city with a patronizing attitude. From one perspective, that is a very good thing; but it falls far short of the example of Christ and the character of His kingdom. If there is anything about the kingdom that we know for sure, it's that at the end of time on this earth, we will all stand before the judgment seat of Jesus Christ. On that day, kings and millionaires will be indistinguishable from slaves and paupers. All whites must learn to receive minorities as equal peers, whether they are stock brokers or minimum wage workers. In some cases, the proud, superior mentality is so ingrained that it's difficult for them to sense the Holy Spirit dealing with their hearts on this issue.

Paul's little letter to Philemon is an example of what the Holy

Spirit wants to do. The epistle to Philemon contains no doctrinal statements or instructions. It is the only surviving piece of Paul's correspondence that is of a purely personal nature. The apostle was writing from a prison cell in Rome to an old friend—a well-to-do gentile businessman whom he had won to Christ. The church in the city met in Philemon's house, so it must have been rather large. One of Philemon's slaves, a man by the name of Onesimus, had stolen some money and run away. For such an offense, a slave would usually be executed. Onesimus somehow wound up in Rome, and as providence would have it, he ran into his master's old friend, the apostle Paul. There, the thief and runaway slave became a Christian and a valuable servant to Paul. After a period of time, though, Paul felt it necessary to send Onesimus back to Philemon, who had every right under Roman law to put him to death, no questions asked. The epistle to Philemon is the letter Paul sent with Onesimus. After a greeting, Paul wrote:

> [8]*Therefore, though I have enough confidence in Christ to order you to do that which is proper,* [9]*yet for love's sake I rather appeal to you—since I am such a person as Paul, the aged, and now also a prisoner of Christ Jesus—*[10]*I appeal to you for my child, whom I have begotten in my imprisonment, Onesimus,* [11]*who formerly was useless to you, but now is useful both to you and to me.*

> [12]*And I have sent him back to you in person, that is, sending my very heart,* [13]*whom I wished to keep with me, that in your behalf he might minister to me in my imprisonment for the gospel;* [14]*but without your consent I did not want to do anything, that your goodness should not be as it were by compulsion, but of your own free will.*

> [15]*For perhaps he was for this reason parted from you for a*
> *while, that you should have him back forever,* [16]*no longer*
> *as a slave, but more than a slave, a beloved brother, espe-*
> *cially to me, but how much more to you, both in the flesh*
> *and in the Lord.* [17]*If then you regard me a partner, accept*
> *him as you would me.* (*Philem. 8–17* NAS)

The purpose of this letter was to appeal to Philemon to overlook the most serious crime of ancient law and take Onesimus back, not as a slave but as a brother. *Treat him just as you would treat me*, said Paul. The apostle was asking a lot, and he knew it. But he was never more serious about anything he said. Though his tone was gracious, notice the pressure he applied in the next two verses:

> [18]*But if he has wronged you in any way, or owes you any-*
> *thing, charge that to my account;* [19]*I, Paul, am writing this*
> *with my own hand, I will repay it (lest I should mention to*
> *you that you owe to me even your own self as well).*
>
> (Philem. 18–19 NAS)

Paul had accepted the thief and runaway slave as a peer, and in no uncertain terms, demanded that Philemon, Onesimus' old master, do the same. The language of Paul's appeal suggests that he knew Philemon was a man who was not predisposed to overlooking such actions, much less to receiving a criminal as a brother.

Things happen in the kingdom that happen nowhere else because the presence of God is there. Think about these three men: a bigoted Jew who was a member of the most exclusive, prejudicial sect on earth;

a gentile businessman who was a pagan idol-worshipper; and a runaway slave. God put them on an equal footing, as brothers in Christ. *That* is the testimony of kingdom diversity the world needs to see!

You might ask, "How do we know that Paul's appeal worked and that Philemon accepted Onesimus as a brother?" It's simple. The letter survived. If Philemon had not responded to Paul's letter, we would not have it today.

5. *Establish a Representative Leadership Structure.*

Leadership in the early church reflected the character of several types of government. Sometimes the foundation of leadership was an appointment from above. Jesus chose disciples, and Paul appointed elders in Galatia (Acts 14:23). At other times the function and foundation of leadership was that of a representative of the people.

When dealing with problems that stemmed from diverse groups within the church, the apostles sensed that it was time to raise up new leaders. The apostles said, *"Select from among you, brethren, seven men of good reputation, full of the Spirit and of wisdom"* (Acts 6:3 NAS). These were not "token Greeks," but men who possessed the qualifications for leadership. In this situation, leaders were chosen as representatives of the congregation.

In the church, we should not appoint or elect unqualified leaders simply to make a statement. At the same time, we must refuse to give place to any prejudicial attitude that will keep us from recognizing minorities whom the Holy Spirit is raising up to represent various segments in the church. *"Do not lay hands upon anyone too hastily"* (1 Tim. 5:22 NAS) is another way of saying "Be very careful about choosing leadership." Laying hands on or commissioning someone for leadership or ministry as merely a *show of diversity* is a well-intentioned act, but it's one that can backfire on you. If, on the other hand, a church sends out signals that only certain types of people are recognized as being qualified for leadership, service, or ministry, this will not go unnoticed. From the greeters at the doors of Christ Church to the senior leadership, we try to display the kind of diversity that is representative of our church.

The most important thing to remember is that unless the Lord builds the house, those who build it labor in vain (Ps. 127:1). God is more interested in demonstrating His kingdom on earth, as it is in heaven, than you are. Jesus told us to pray for the Lord of the harvest to send forth laborers. God Himself will raise up a diverse, representative leadership for any congregation that desires to obey the Lord's commission to disciple the nations.

Toward the end of the first century, Ignatius, the bishop of the church of Antioch, was taken under guard to Rome, where he would become a martyr for Christ. Since the Egnatian Way did not go through Ephesus, the church sent a delegation to meet him. In response to this warm reception, Ignatius wrote a letter to the Ephesian church.

> For you were all zeal to visit me when you heard that I was being shipped as a prisoner from Syria for the sake of our common Name and hope. I hope, indeed, by your prayers to have the good fortune to fight with the wild beasts in Rome, so that by doing this I can be a real disciple. In God's name, therefore, I received your large congregation in the person of *Onesimus* [italics added], your bishop in this world, a man whose love is beyond words. My prayer is that you should love him in the spirit of Jesus Christ and all like him. Blessed is He who let you have such a bishop. You deserve it.[1]

It is not certain whether this Onesimus was the slave who fifty years earlier had run away from Philemon and become a servant and disciple of Paul. Many scholars believe he was. Whether or not this was the same Onesimus doesn't matter. The point is that it *could have been*, because that's just the kind of thing God does in the kingdom. He'll take the runaway slave, save him, and raise him up to be bishop of one of the greatest churches in Christendom.

—————Chapter 10—————

CROSS-CULTURAL WORSHIP

How do you treat the subject of worship in a congregation composed of blacks, whites, Hispanics, Asians, and a dozen other ethnic groups? Worship is one of the most controversial subjects in a cross-cultural environment. What type of music should be played? Should the rhythm be fast, slow, moderate, or a combination of the three? Should the music have a jazz, calypso, rock, soft rock, classical, salsa, reggae, southern gospel, traditional, or contemporary flavor? How do you accommodate various groups with a diversity of music and still have a great worship experience? These are tough questions, but keep this in mind: If the church's mission is to harvest people for Christ in a community that is growing increasingly diverse, then the Holy Spirit undoubtedly will show a way to those who seek Him with open hearts and minds.

Most people approach worship from a selfish perspective. Their primary concern is how they can touch God and receive His touch. It's a valid personal concern, but one that can isolate the worshipper from the needs of the broader church community. Private worship is distinctly different from corporate worship. Worship in a private setting deals strictly with the individual's communion with God.

Our private devotional habits, such as our worship posture, our favorite songs, and our devotional structure, are developed early in our

Christian experience. When no one else is there watching except the Lord, you should take advantage of the freedom to enjoy yourself in whatever way God leads you. But our tendency is to prefer the same agenda for corporate worship that we've adopted for our private times with the Lord. Some people even demand this. For many people, corporate worship is in essence like having private devotions in a crowd. But the Holy Spirit has much more in mind for the church.

Seventy-nine percent of American churchgoers worship in a monoracial setting.[1] (Please refer to Table 1 on page 85.) Much of what people have been taught or simply assume about worship is not completely biblical. If your experience has only been in a monocultural setting, you will probably have a very limited perspective. Thus, in order to establish a model for worship that is corporate, inclusive, and personally fulfilling, we need to take a fresh look at the biblical pattern.

WHAT IS WORSHIP?

Robert E. Webber articulated one of the best definitions of worship that I've come across. Webber studied the worship habits of different denominations, movements, and cultural groups. In his book *Worship Old and New*, he wrote:

> Worship is the enactment of an event (Christ-event), the organization of worship is not left to the whim of creative people or community consensus. Christian worship derives from the death and resurrection of Christ. In preaching we retell the story, in the Eucharist we dramatize the event. Even worship on Sunday has significance in terms of enactment, for this is the day of the Resurrection.[2]

Worship, therefore, is a proclamation. When the body of Christ gathers, the gospel message should be clearly proclaimed through our worship, regardless of the particular musical style. All those present at corporate worship, whether or not they are Christians, should walk away from the meeting with a fresh understanding (or even a *first* understanding) of the atoning death of Jesus, which satisfied God's wrath against sinful man. They should hear of the Christ-event and the good news of what it means for each person.

This proclamation is simply a response to God. John Burkhart, a professor of theology, writes, "Fundamentally, worship is the celebrative response to what God has done, is doing, and promises to do."[3]

Worship also entails reaching out to God to fill the hunger in the soul of man. Nothing stops starving and thirsty people from doing what it takes to get their basic needs met. The Scriptures use this metaphor to describe the soul's desperation to touch God. The psalmist David wrote, "O God, you are my God, earnestly I seek you; my soul thirsts for you, my body longs for you, in a dry and weary land where there is no water" (Ps. 63:1). David penned this psalm in the desert of Judah while he was agonizing over his imminent capture. Judson Cornwall, a noted author on the subject of worship, comments:

> This deep longing after God seems rare in our generation,
> or at least we don't seem to discern it to be the craving of
> our spirits after the Spirit of God. We tend to think that it is
> our soul wanting amusement or our body craving food or
> exercise; but David was sufficiently tuned into his spirit to
> recognize deep longings after God.[4]

In a stricter and more technical sense, the meaning of worship is expressed in the Greek word *proskuneo*, which means "to prostrate oneself in homage; to do reverence; to adore." The word suggests honor and submission, as in a dog fawning, crouching in front of, or licking the hand of its master. Thus, when we worship, we adore the Lord in the humblest of ways. The word "worship" can be traced to the Old English word "worth-ship." Christian worship is expressed by loving, adoring, and giving glory to God for His intrinsic value.

If worship is an act of service to God, then our worship must always be in sync with the desires of God as recorded in sacred Scripture. He desires *"all men to be saved and to come to a knowledge of the truth"* (1 Tim. 2:4). So, worship must be conducted in a manner that's inclusive of "all men." In order to accomplish this, we need to carefully think through the dynamics of culturally inclusive worship.

How Do You Shop?

In sixteen years of marriage, I've learned that, like most men and women, my wife and I shop very differently. For most men, shopping is a hunt, while for most women it's like going on a safari.

A few years ago, I was out of town for a speaking engagement. When early the first morning I realized I had forgotten to pack extra shirts, I immediately set out for the nearest mall. The men's store had not yet opened when I arrived, but a man was already standing there, anxiously waiting. As soon as the door was unlocked, he rushed in and announced with great urgency that he needed a white shirt, a blue suit, and a pair of shoes.

"Any particular style of suit?" the salesperson asked.

"Anything! Just hurry!" said the man, who seemed quite put out that the salesman should waste his time by asking. In less than fifteen minutes, my fellow hunter was in and out, having bagged his trophy. I was a bit slower to slay my shirts. But in another five minutes, I was out of there too.

I remember the first couple of shopping safaris on which my wife took me after we got married. From one store to the next she would go—window shopping, browsing, pricing, looking for bargains, and trying on dresses, shoes, and blouses. I'm one of those people who evaluate a shopping trip with a mathematical formula: the number of items purchased, divided by the number of minutes spent, equals the shopping efficiency quotient. A shopping safari is a big test for a newly wed husband.

On another occasion, I went to the mall with Marlinda to look for a pair of shoes. We were both very busy, so I figured this would be a good opportunity to spend some time together. After she tried on perhaps fifteen to twenty pairs of shoes in four or five different stores, I just couldn't take it any longer. Exhausted and impatient, I cried, "Honey, no more stores! No more trying on shoes! We're buying right now!" I took out my checkbook and bought seven different colored pairs of shoes, all in the style she was trying on at the moment.

Marlinda couldn't understand what I was so upset about. Safari shopping was what she was used to. Reflecting back, I recalled how my mother and sister used to shop when I was a boy. They all used the safari style. There wasn't much I could do about it then. But as an adult I had vowed to never again allow myself to be dragged from store to store on one of these shopping excursions.

After the first few years of marriage, I did come to appreciate my wife's shopping style. This change of attitude is mostly because I love her and want to show deference to her. What makes a great marriage is not that two people are exactly alike. It's that each has learned to appreciate and accommodate the uniqueness of God's gift in the other. Though

I am not a safari-style shopper and will never be one, my change of heart has enabled me to accept that style of shopping. The fact that I made big mistakes on several of my shopping hunts has had a lot to do with my newfound appreciation for the way my wife does things.

Cross-cultural worship reminds me a lot of our shopping habits. Our love for fellow church members should move the worship experience away from selfishness toward accommodation. I could have easily adopted an attitude of self-righteousness and stubbornness regarding shopping style. But I would have alienated Marlinda in the process. This is what happens in so many houses of worship. We build cultural barricades between one another all because we're just too selfish. True love looks to build bridges and to establish common ground. The Christ-event is the most common of all grounds on which one stands as a Christian. When worship is built on our response to God and upon the foundation of the death, burial, and resurrection of Christ, our corporate worship experience will naturally draw *all* people together as they draw closer to Him.

"HELP! I CAN'T MOVE TO THE BEAT OF THE MUSIC!"

I have been told by Hispanics, African-Americans, Asians, and even whites, "David, you don't have any rhythm. You can't even clap on the beat."

My response has always been, "Leave me alone! I'm making a joyful noise unto the Lord."

Music, worship, and culture are all interconnected. Think about the church where you learned various worship postures and habits. Did you not follow the cultural traditions of that congregation and its pastor? I started this chapter by saying that most Christians' worship habits are culturally learned and not necessarily strictly biblical. There is no precisely right or wrong way to worship God. The problem is that people think of their own style as "the Bible way." The Samaritan woman at the well posed the question to Jesus about whose place and method of worship was right in God's eyes. The ingredients of biblical worship are found in Jesus' simple reply: *"God is spirit, and his worshipers must worship in spirit and in truth"* (John 4:24).

The God of the Bible is the one true God. It is He who created the heavens and the earth. The Westminster *Confession of Faith* answers the question concerning the acceptable way of worship: "The only acceptable way of worshipping God is that given in the Scriptures and requires the mediation of Christ."[5]

Comprehending the degree to which our culture affects us is difficult. It is woven into every facet of what we do, like a well-tailored garment that cannot be separated from its wearer. But the role that culture plays in our lives must be recognized and understood if we are to lead or participate in cross-cultural worship. H. Richard Niebuhr, in the classic work *Christ and Culture,* defines culture this way:

[It is] the work of men's minds and hands. It is that portion of man's heritage in any place or time which has been given us designedly and laboriously by other men, not what has come to us via the mediation of nonhuman beings or through human beings insofar as they have acted without intention of results or without control of the process. Hence it includes speech, education, tradition, myth, science, art, philosophy, government, law, rite, beliefs, inventions, technologies.[6]

To a great degree, each person has been scripted by his culture, imprinted with desires and preferences. In my culture, hot foods are preferred over cold foods, even if it's 85 degrees outside! In the summer, I'll eat hot sandwiches for lunch while everyone else eats cold cuts. My eating habits don't make any more sense to my wife than her safari shopping does to me. But we don't have to change the way we are in order to live together in harmony.

Each one of us grew up within a certain musical environment. More than likely, it was someone from that same environment who introduced us to Christ. According to C. Peter Wagner in *Church Growth: The State of the Art*, "Eighty-six percent of new people brought into the church come through friends and relatives."[7] Christians in monocultural churches tend to "beget" new Christians and new members from their own peer groups—people who were raised in similar cultures with similar musical preferences.

To break this culturally exclusive cycle, Christians must broaden their circles of friends, both numerically and ethnically. We simply have to get out of the box in which we've grown up. When people begin to explore the world outside their familiar confines, they learn to appreciate the musical styles and preferences of their brothers and sisters in Christ.

PASTOR, WE NEED YOUR LEADERSHIP

The local church is a unique organism. For the most part, churches reflect the character, vision, values, and the philosophy of ministry of the senior pastor. People will join a particular church partly because they feel they can accept the pastor as their role model. Parishioners make both verbal and nonverbal commitments to follow the pastor as the pastor follows Christ.

Show me a cross-cultural pastor, and I'll show you a cross-cultural congregation. Show me a pastor whose personal life has an abundance of diversity, and I'll show you a pastor whose public life calls for the same requirements. The pastor sets the pace for the congregation and helps them develop a taste for what he prefers in worship, as well as in other areas of the Christian faith.

In *A Shepherd Looks at Psalm 23*, Philip Keller speaks to this point from his vocational experience as a shepherd. He writes:

> Because of the behavior of sheep and their preference for certain favored spots [grazing areas], these well-worn areas become quickly infested with parasites of all kinds. In a short time a whole flock can thus become infested with worms, nematodes and scab. The final upshot is that both land and owner are ruined while the sheep become thin, wasted and sickly.
>
> The greatest safeguard a shepherd has in handling his flock is to keep them on the move. That is to say, they dare not be left on the same ground too long. They must be shifted from pasture to pasture periodically. This prevents over-grazing of the forage. It also avoids the rutting of trails and erosion of land from over-use. It forestalls the re-infestation of the sheep with internal parasites or disease, since the sheep move off the infested ground before these organisms complete their life cycles.
>
> In a word—there must be a pre-determined plan of action, a deliberate, planned rotation from one grazing ground to another in line with right and proper principles of sound management.[8]

Keller's elaboration on the duty of a shepherd with regard to the needs and care of the sheep reflects both a preventative and a visionary leadership style. Verse 3 of Psalm 23 reads, *"[My shepherd] guides me in paths of righteousness for his name's sake."* In a strictly theological sense, the phrase refers to the Lord, our Chief Shepherd. In a broader interpretation, the passage also refers to local "under-shepherds." I understand this verse to mean that as a local pastor, I have the responsibility to lead my parishioners in healthy, life-giving ways that embody righteousness. If I don't do this, the unhealthy state of my congregation will be a reflection of my poor management and leadership skills. My responsibility is to do this "for His name's sake." God's name would be held in disrepute if He were an unfaithful shepherd. How much more are local pastors to be held accountable for providing adequate care for the sheep with whom they've been entrusted?

In the local church, the flow of truth originates with the Holy Spirit and flows through the pastor to the congregation. Pastors are trainers, equippers, modelers, coaches, disciplinarians, and facilitators of truth. Sheep look for direction and leadership from their shepherds. The music department, as well as the entire worship atmosphere of a church, must be shepherded by its pastors.

But we cannot place ultimate responsibility on the shoulders of pastors. Each person has to give an account for himself when the time comes for all to stand before the judgment seat of Christ. At that point, we can't say, "My pastor didn't teach me about appreciating different types of people. That's why I didn't accept others." Jesus would simply remind us of this statement: *"As for you, the anointing you received from [Christ] remains in you, and you do not need anyone to teach you. But as his anointing teaches you about all things and as that anointing is real, not counterfeit—just as it has taught you, remain in him"* (1 John 2:27).

Every one of us is without excuse when it comes to modeling *agape* love and fostering inclusion in every area of our lives. The Lord has already stated His position on the matter. It is indisputable!

THE DYNAMICS OF CROSS-CULTURAL WORSHIP

Worship is not just the thirty minutes or so of praise songs that most churches sing. Worship is the entire encounter we have with God when we gather corporately. Robert Webber writes:

> I have discovered that worship is best understood when it carries the worshipper through a sequence of related events such as: (1) preparation to worship, (2) reading and preaching the word, (3) Holy Communion, and (4) Dismissal. In this sequence, the story of our coming to God—of hearing him speak, of entering into communion with him and of being sent forth is the order of worship.[9]

Although I will limit my discussion to the singing and musical components of cross-cultural worship, please understand that the principles cited are applicable to all the other parts of our corporate worship service. Preaching, teaching, drama, the administration of the gifts of the Spirit, and so forth are all components of worship. To have a thorough sense of inclusion, diversity must be the hallmark of every area of ministry.

People love to be in an environment where love thrives. Love a person, and he will always want to spend time with you. There are several ingredients needed in order to adopt a cross-cultural style of worship where love is present and the Christ-event is the reason for the gathering.

Cross-cultural worship is a window into the transcendent nature of God. Transcendence speaks of God existing apart from the material universe—beyond the limits of the created world. It reflects God's nature as surpassing, excelling, and reaching beyond the limits of the ordinary into the extraordinary. Thus, cross-cultural worship should be extraordinary because of the following realities:

1. Cross-Cultural Worship Reaches Beyond the Preferences of Each Culture.

In corporate worship, the people's attention should be on the whole, rather than on the individual parts. Singing songs, preaching the Word, and other worship components are focused on the whole body receiving from the Holy Spirit. Individual cultural preferences must be subordinated to the whole church in order to touch the heart of God. People have to be trained to follow the guidance of the Holy Spirit in corporate meetings, sometimes against their learned behavior or cultural scripting.

Worshippers must realize that patience is a fruit of the Spirit. Sometimes the Holy Spirit anoints a particular song that some people just don't get anything out of. In a large family, the members must be gracious when their brothers' and sisters' needs are being met and theirs aren't. Next week, your needs may be powerfully met, while your neighbor works through the same issues you dealt with the week before.

Cross-cultural worship must transcend the preferences of each culture—both the majority and the minorities. Biblical Christianity presents a dynamic type of corporate worship that can only be embraced when a person realizes that the part he plays is not more important than the whole. This viewpoint becomes a reality when change is embraced. And since change is introduced to a person, and ultimately to the entire church body, biblical worship resists being restricted, confined, or suppressed by narrow ethnocentrism. Our ethnicity does not and should not subordinate the expression of the Holy Spirit.

Since our church is composed of approximately 5 to 10 percent Hispanics, we have learned to sing some worship choruses in Spanish. It was a struggle at first to sing in Spanish. I always jokingly say that I can hardly speak English, much less Spanish. You should have seen and heard our worship team singing in Spanish the first time we tried

it. A Hispanic couple in the congregation were getting married immediately following the morning service. To make it easy on their friends
and relatives, they had invited their guests to our Sunday service. Since
I was involved in the planning, I asked the worship team to share one of
the Spanish songs that Sunday.

When the day came, quite a number of Latinos were present for
the worship service. About halfway through our time of worship, we
started singing the Spanish song. I looked around to see how people
were responding. To my delight, one of the elderly Hispanic ladies had
tears streaming down her face. The tears represented two things: 1) the
nonreligious people in the group saw how they mattered to God; and,
2) they realized how much they mattered to us because they recognized
that we had planned for their visit beforehand.

My worship experience that day soared to new heights of personal gratification. Our desire to be true to our vision of inclusion allowed our worship to reach beyond many of the cultural walls to touch
a culture that had little representation in our church family. I honestly
believe that God was pleased with our efforts that day.

2. Cross-Cultural Worship Reaches Beyond the Dominant Culture Within the Congregation.

When you look around at your church family, one culture may
stand out more than the rest. The majority's preference is not necessarily the will of God, nor is it the choice of the Holy Spirit on any particular occasion as you gather for worship. Paul established the principle of
sensitivity with this statement:

> [12]*The body is a unit, though it is made up of many parts;
> and though all its parts are many, they form one body....*[21]*The*

eye cannot say to the hand, "I don't need you!" And the head cannot say to the feet, "I don't need you!" [22]On the contrary, those parts of the body that seem to be weaker are indispensable.... (1 Cor. 12:12, 21–22)

It takes a mature Christian to recognize that the majority's preference is not always the Holy Spirit's preference. God is into inclusion, not exclusion. I'm not suggesting that the needs of the majority should be unmet or ignored. Spirit-directed worship is satisfying to everyone. Even the unchurched person can walk away from a worship service feeling somewhat inspired, or at best, challenged to reevaluate the spiritual direction of his or her life.

A few years ago, I spoke at a worship conference in Atlantic City, New Jersey. One of the evening meetings was held in a large auditorium on the boardwalk. When the service began, voices filled the air with joyous praise. Lovers walking down the boardwalk holding hands came into the meeting to enjoy the sounds and sights of worship. People walking dogs came right inside the doorway and watched. Their dogs sat and watched us praise God. It was a sight to behold. Biblical worship is inclusive and entreats all to receive from God.

If the cultural majority of the church desires to grow in diversity and inclusion, a spirit of accommodation must radiate from the hearts of these people and translate into transcendent worship. Cross-cultural worship must go beyond the walls of the culture of the majority and allow others to enjoy the presence of a loving, caring, inclusive God.

3. Cross-Cultural Worship Reaches Beyond the Generation Gaps.

The congregational makeup of many churches is "generationally skewed." By that I mean that the overwhelming majority of the people are from the same generation. Some churches are composed of people almost all of whom are over fifty-five years old. Others have congregations in which almost all are under age forty. The church needs a strong representation from every generation because there are values and traditions that can be easily lost if our grandparents and parents do not pass them down. Paul told Titus:

> *³Likewise, teach the older women to be reverent in the way they live, not to be slanderers or addicted to much wine, but to teach what is good. ⁴Then they can train the younger women to love their husbands and children, ⁵to be self-controlled and pure, to be busy at home, to be kind, and to be subject to their husbands, so that no one will malign the word of God.* (Titus 2:3–5)

I wonder how many divorces and other social maladies could be avoided if there were effective communication and an ongoing discipleship relationship between the older and younger generations.

The element of care must become interwoven into the fabric of our worship. Paul wrote, *"But if a widow has children or grandchildren, these should learn first of all to put their religion into practice by caring for their own family and so repaying their parents and grandparents, for this is pleasing to God"* (1 Tim. 5:4). Sensitivity to the needs of each generation must become an outworking of our devotion to God. If this commandment is not obeyed, the church will be a fragmented community, and the gospel will not have a transgenerational impact.

This transgenerational sensitivity must work both ways. The older generations need the enthusiasm, freshness, and zeal of the youth. "Boomers," "Busters," "Generation X-ers," and everyone in between have a special place in the church, as do their worship preferences. But if the elders religiously impose their preferences on the young people, they will almost always lose that generation as soon as they are old enough to choose according to their own preferences. Our teenagers and children will never see themselves as the church of the future if church involvement simply means acting like an old person. There is no thought more horrifying to a teenager.

The church must take a proactive approach to incorporating music styles from every generation. If the elders and music leaders refuse to change until they receive a large enough number of complaints about generational or cultural insensitivity, it will almost always be too late. People vote with their feet, and even those who are slow to leave will "check out" emotionally. Imagine all the huge cathedrals and fabulous buildings that are empty every week—or that have only fifty to seventy-five elderly people scattered among the empty pews. These are usually good people who love God very much, but they and their leadership have missed the transcendent purpose of God in worship. The attendance of these churches declined because they were no longer culturally and generationally relevant.

Most readers can probably relate to the fact that the church will lose kids if the older generation is not attuned to the younger generation's cultural preferences. But the same thing is true of cultural, ethnic, educational, and socioeconomic diversity. That's why every aspect of church life must present a transcendent view of God that is both transgenerational and multicultural. And how you view God as a church becomes most evident in the method, style, and content of your worship.

I struggled for almost a year at Christ Church to impart to the congregation an appreciation for the great hymns of the church. I wanted everyone to understand that different musical styles were equal entry points to a meaningful worship experience. Most people seemed to be simply tolerating the pastor, thinking that if they just waited long enough, I would sooner or later move on to another topic. But they had no intention of embracing traditional hymns. Though I did not give up on the notion of hymns being included in a diverse worship experience, I did eventually move on to other topics.

Several months later, when I was preaching on the value and richness of our Christian heritage, we sang a few hymns, but still without any enthusiasm. It was as if the people were singing as their obligatory good deed for the day. Normally, worship at Christ Church is very vibrant, expressive, and celebrative. So to see the congregation worship in an uncharacteristically melancholy way was upsetting.

Finally, after much prayer and teaching, along with a lot of practice on the part of the worship team, we had a significant breakthrough. I can remember the Sunday when we sang "A Mighty Fortress Is Our God." The power of God in the room was electric! The people were weeping as the Holy Spirit reminded them that God is indeed a mighty fortress in our daily lives. This wasn't a newly acquired appreciation of a musical style; it was a generational breakthrough.

Throughout the twelve-month ordeal, the older people in the church were enjoying the hymns, but the majority of the people, who were younger than fifty years old, struggled to see the value. As the shepherd of the flock, I led them with the rod and the staff. Since sheep would rather graze where they are, there was a lot of resistance along the way. And it's always easier for the shepherd to just go with what the sheep want. But through it all, we were able to move to greener pastures. As a result, our worship is much better, much fresher, much deeper, and transgenerational in style.

4. Cross-Cultural Worship Must Touch the Heart of God.

David, the psalmist of Israel, was one of the most passionate worshippers who ever lived. He wasn't ashamed to worship God passionately in public. His desire was to touch the heart of God. To him, worship was no one else's business. It was between a servant and his Master.

This is what true worshippers desire to do—to unabashedly boast about their God. David wrote, *"From you comes the theme of my praise in the great assembly; before those who fear you will I fulfill my vows"* (Ps. 22:25). Although his worship was private, his feelings for God were too big to be contained or concealed. He had to go public with his innermost thoughts about God. He sang, *"I will declare your name to my brothers; in the congregation I will praise you"* (Ps. 22:22). Our worship must take on this attitude.

Cross-cultural worship is not an innovation of twenty-first-century Christians. It's the same extraordinary, dynamic, heartfelt worship that the patriarchs offered to a transcendent God. David prayed, *"All the nations you have made will come and worship before you, O Lord; they will bring glory to your name. For you are great and do marvelous deeds; you alone are God"* (Ps. 86:9–10). Can you imagine this vivid scene: Hispanics, blacks, whites, Asians, Indians, and those of other races worshipping together before the Lord? This is the heart of cross-cultural worship: all nations responding to God and to one another.

Only God can accomplish this feat. Our hearts, however, must be open for change. If you love God, you must also love His creation. Start by trying to understand how to love people. It's just like a marriage. My wife had to teach me how to love and respond to her. Similarly, I had to teach her how to respond in such a way that I could feel her love for me.

Cross-cultural worship calls for us to move out of our comfort zones to touch both God and one another. Start by simply trying to understand. Listen to different radio stations that feature the music of various ethnic groups. Try it! Include prayer in the process. Ask God to open your heart to an appreciation of people—all kinds of people. Talk with your pastor and music leaders about including a broader array of music in the worship repertoire. Remember, Scripture teaches, *"The prayer of a righteous man is powerful and effective"* (James 5:16b). Bathe your efforts in prayer, and watch what God will do.

———*Chapter 11*———

CROSS-CULTURAL
RELATIONSHIPS

T here is a growing percentage of the U.S. population whose
genealogies resemble that of Eldrick "Tiger" Woods, who calls
himself a "Caublinasian." Woods uses this self-crafted acro-
nym to represent his heritage as one-eighth Caucasian, one-fourth black,
one-eighth American Indian, one-fourth Thai, and one-fourth Chinese.

In 1950, the classification of "other" consisted of slightly more
than one million people—less than 1 percent of the population. In 1995,
there were almost twelve million people in the United States—4.5 percent of the population—who identified themselves as neither black nor
white.[1] Since 1970, the number of multiracial children has quadrupled
to more than two million. This demographic trend is called by sociologists "the browning of America."[2]

In the last twenty-five years, the percentage of the foreign-born
population in the United States has doubled, from 4.8 percent in 1970
to 8.8 percent in 1997. The most rapid of all growth is in races other
than black or white. Though the percentage of the population that is
black has grown steadily (from 9.9 percent in 1950 to 12.7 percent in
1995), by the mid-twenty-first century Hispanics will have overtaken
blacks as the largest minority.

America has always been a nation of racial and ethnic diversity.
This diversity has also been accompanied by prejudice, an attitude that

173

always gives birth to segregation. In the oldest cities of America, neighborhoods are still divided into exclusively ethnic sectors—Italian, Polish, Jewish, Chinese, Korean, and so on. As each racial and ethnic minority gains a larger slice of America's "cultural market share," the Anglo-Saxon white majority, once completely dominant, will eventually have to relate to other races on an equal footing socially, economically, and politically.

As a nation and as the church, we must take the issue of racism very seriously. When the victims of racism comprise a relatively small minority, they can be easily overlooked. But soon this will no longer be the case. We will not be able to ignore the problem of racism. We must learn to live together in unity now.

INTERRACIAL RELATIONSHIPS

The question of interracial marriages is usually ground zero in any honest discussion about cross-cultural relationships. It's been my experience that not everyone who attends an interracial church supports interracial dating and marriage. But we cannot fully espouse the doctrine of reconciliation and at the same time place rigid boundaries around the issue of relationships.

If you agree that no boundaries should exist in platonic friendships, then there should also be no restrictions regarding romantic relationships. If you're going to preach reconciliation, you need to do it consistently.

Please do not read into my statements that I'm equating reconciliation with interracial marriage. Reconciliation in the generic sense has to do with people loving, respecting, accommodating, and socializing with people who are racially, culturally, socioeconomically, and ethnically different from themselves. Miscegenation, or interracial marriage, is the marriage of two people of different races. Reconciliation and interracial marriage are two entirely different subjects. But they must be discussed in light of the way God fitted us together as human beings. We are creatures of love, and we cannot shut down or turn off the emotions that guide us in selecting lifelong marriage partners because of the sociological hang-ups of others.

A world-class Christian cannot aggressively pursue the lost with the message of God's inclusive love for mankind and in the same breath say, "but God doesn't want us to marry each other if we are from different races." When you step back and take a look at such a statement, you can see that it is an unsound position.

The historical arguments, which many continue to parrot, are neither scriptural nor valid. If you support racial reconciliation, then you cannot quarantine singles to make sure they don't fall in love with people of another race. Couples like Moses and Zipporah (Num. 12:1–3), Rahab and Salmon (Matt. 1:5), Ruth and Boaz (Ruth 4:10), and David and Bathsheba (2 Sam. 11:27) had interracial, or at the very least bicultural, marriages. The implication of Scripture is that God did not disapprove.

Moses was Jewish, and his wife, Zipporah, was a Cushite. Some Bible translations use the word *Ethiopian,* while others use the word *Cushite.* The Cushites were descendents of Cush (Noah's grandson); they inhabited ancient Ethiopia, the country of the blacks. Rahab was a former Canaanite prostitute who lived in Jericho before it was destroyed by Joshua and his army (Josh. 6:17). Her husband, Salmon, was an Israelite to whom she was married after the defeat of Jericho. Incidentally, Boaz was the son of the union of Salmon and Rahab (Ruth 4:21; Matt. 1:5), and his union with Ruth was blessed by the birth of Obed, the grandfather of David. Ruth was a Moabite woman, while Boaz was a bicultural Jew. David, the second Jewish king and the grandson of a bicultural union married a woman named Bathsheba ("daughter of the oath"), who most scholars believe was a black woman. Jesus came from the lineage of David. Jesus the Christ was born a Jew, but had a cross-cultural bloodline.

This diversity in the ancestry of Jesus makes it clear that He came to save *all* of mankind. Before we delve further into the subject of interracial marriages, I must make clear that people who marry outside of the direction of the Holy Spirit, for self-esteem purposes, or in rebellion have a very difficult hill to climb in achieving marital bliss. Some people marry outside of their race simply because they suffer from low self-esteem and consider it advantageous to marry someone from a race that traditionally ranks on a higher social level than their own. Premarital counseling should weed out such motives and give a strong warning to those making such a decision.

In an interracial church, marrying someone who is different from you may seem fashionable. In some cases, the couples involved in interracial romances are simply rebelling against God. There are also times when the rebellion is against family members, friends, or even society.

Whether the reason individuals decide to wed outside their race is because they want to go against the grain of society, try something different, or prove a point to their parents, they are still in rebellion. Deep down they know that the relationship is not of the Holy Spirit. Unfortunately, they pay a high price for this rebellion. Obedience to God and acceptance of His choice in a marriage partner are very serious issues. World-class churches must instruct singles to select spouses for reasons that glorify God and make for good lifelong marriages.

"People Don't Understand My Marriage"

Twenty-first-century churches must learn to accept interracial relationships on all levels if they are to be relevant and accommodating to the ethnic groups moving into their neighborhoods. Frequent stares and inappropriate questions make racially blended couples feel alienated in their communities and churches.

"We feel as if we're a project that the church members don't understand," said the husband of an interracial couple. "Their questions and their body language make us feel very awkward," he added. In an ideal world, this interracial couple would have preferred that their church family accept their unique relationship and get on with the business of making disciples for Christ. A world-class Christian simply views interracial couples as potential candidates for the kingdom of God, who are just as deserving of love as anyone else.

What About New Members?

Overcoming monoculturalism on an organizational level is one thing; dealing with it on an individual level is another thing entirely. We all bring the baggage of prejudice and victimization into the kingdom of God. The love of God must wash us, and His grace must ready us for true community living. World-class churches fight this battle daily. Each new member that is added to the local church must be introduced to the things that God has already imparted to the church. At Christ Church, we begin at square one with each new group of members, sharing with them this sentiment: *God has called us to be reconciled to one another.* Annually, I teach a series of messages for new people on how to become Christlike in their behaviors and attitudes toward their brothers and sisters of a different hue. At the same time, I remind the existing members to strengthen their commitment to biblical reconciliation. A lifelong dedication to God's desire for a cross-cultural, racially diverse local church requires constant inspection, supervision, and maintenance.

"Can You Love Our Bi-racial Children?"

An interracial couple in our congregation shared one of their challenges with me concerning their preschooler. The husband is an African-American, and the wife is of German descent. Their pretty little daughter has light brown skin and long brunette hair. At her Christian preschool, the other little children kept asking Tara if her mother was really her mother. The mother is a very tall, attractive, blonde woman. Tara often asked her in private, "Mom, are you really my mom?" The reply was always, "Honey, you are God's special gift to Daddy and me." As this little girl grew, she overcame the imposing questions of her cultural identity. As an older child, Tara wrote the following poem, which was printed by a local newspaper.

Are You Really My Mother?

Are you really my mother?
Friends stop and stare,
Wondering who you are,
Is that your mother, they ask?

I look at your skin, and then at mine,
Why am I brown, while you are white?
Did God mix up the crayons?
Maybe He colored me too dark.

As I have grown I have noticed,
We smile alike, we laugh at the same things,
We possess the same gentleness,
We are connected.

God doesn't make mistakes,
I am an image of you,
I am your daughter,
And you are my mother.[3]

The world-class church must posture itself to be a welcoming community, or we could forfeit the allegiance of the next generation. The browning of America brings with it an increasing number of bi-racial children. We must teach the church family acceptance and the value of diversity. This instruction does not mean that we should treat interracial families as projects. Rather, we must teach people to love one another through our service to God.

The world-class church must celebrate diversity and not simply tolerate it. Jesus was slain and did *"purchase for God with [His] blood men from every tribe and tongue and people and nation"* (Rev. 5:9 NAS). Since Jesus is the Lord of the harvest who chooses every ethnic group to adorn His kingdom, who are we to reject those whom He has so graciously accepted?

As the number of bi-racial children increases, new challenges will arise. Lingenfelter and Mayers addressed the point of procrastination on this matter with these comments:

Individuals as well as cultures differ in their orientation to-ward and management of crisis. Those with a non-crisis orientation tend to take things when they come; they do not expect or look for problems. Those who are crisis-oriented, however, tend to examine every activity for potential flaws or problems. The noncrisis-oriented person tends to be optimistic; the crisis-oriented person, pessimistic.[4]

Whether we view the world from a crisis or a noncrisis perspective, we must create workable strategies for interracial church communities. We have to press toward God through prayer and dialogue around the ethnic roundtable to get answers for the crises of our day. We can't wait for the sociological projections to come true. Let's act now. Our children are at stake.

CULTURAL TRANSITIONS

Several years ago, I took a mission trip to South Africa, which was then under President Botha's reign, just after apartheid had been lifted. Previously, the Christian Afrikaaners had exhibited great faith in God. Nothing had seemed impossible to them. They had built palatial churches with high hopes of reaching other Afrikaaners for Christ. But with the country's uncertain destiny due to the probable shift to African leadership, the Afrikaaners saw God in a slightly different light. They were becoming more cautious in their faith. The pending political transition brought a newfound sobriety.

Cultural transitions are often accompanied by a great deal of stress. In nations where the ascendant majority refuses to be reconciled for fear of losing its grip on society, business, and politics, the pressure always builds until it eventually explodes in upheaval and chaos.

There are two factors that place the church in a unique position for modeling reconciliation and diversity. First, every Christian has a bond with every other Christian that supersedes racial, ethnic, and nationalistic divisions. We are of the same spiritual race (see chapter 4), and we have a common citizenship in heaven. As the apostle Paul put it, *"You are no longer foreigners and aliens, but fellow citizens with God's people and members of God's household, built on the foundation of the apostles and prophets, with Christ Jesus himself as the chief cornerstone"* (Eph. 2:19–20). By the Spirit of God, the ties to our mutual race, citizenship, and family are eternal and outweigh the ties to our earthly race and citizenship.

Secondly, at the end of the twentieth century, the church experienced a profound transformation in its racial and cultural makeup. Though the Christian church began as a sect of Judaism, it soon spread to the gentile world and eventually found its strongest foothold in Europe. From the second century on, the intellectual, political, and cultural influence of the church was based in Europe. But in 1982, the church reached a significant historical milestone that went unnoticed by almost all Christians and churches. For the first time, the majority of professing Christians were nonwhite.

Today, the church of Jesus Christ is mostly Latin American, Asian, and African. Revival is sweeping many of the Third World nations, and the list of new believers is growing. Caucasian Christians are becoming a smaller and smaller minority. Consequently, the Holy Spirit has put the church in the position not only to model racial reconciliation, but also to display the kind of unity and harmony that the world, particularly the United States, will desperately need in the coming years.

Caucasian Christians from the Western world need to realize that most of their brothers and sisters in Christ are black and brown and live in the Third World. If we all can learn to identify, appreciate, and communicate with the family of God around the globe, we will move toward modeling reconciliation and restoration on a local level.

THINKING GLOBALLY

As a Christian, my vision and understanding of the kingdom of God cannot be confined within the walls of Christ Church in Montclair, New Jersey. My concern is for the neighborhoods, the schools, and the city. My burden is for the entire area, the East Coast, the nation, and the nations of the world. Jesus did not say (as some of the Jews would have expected), "For God so loved *Israel* that He gave His only begotten Son..." He gave because He loved the *world*. You can't be like Christ and at the same time love only those in your own little circle. He has called us to disciple the nations.

The opposite of thinking globally is thinking locally and, in the extreme, thinking selfishly. Ecclesiastical self-centeredness has been characterized historically by the European church in the era of "empire building," and by the church in "isolationist America."

The Isolationist Church

Protected on both sides by great oceans, Americans have histori-cally been isolationists. Relatively few Americans speak a second lan-guage, let alone a third or fourth. The isolationist has little concern for the rest of the world or for those of other nations.

Every culture has characteristics that God uses as "redemptive gifts." But these characteristics can also be used in opposition to His purposes. Throughout our nation's history, Americans have been known for their independence and self-reliance. While independence can have positive effects, it can also cause people to isolate themselves within the boundaries of self-interest. Futurist and cultural commentator Faith Popcorn refers to modern expressions of independence and isolation-ism as "cocooning." The trend in American families is to "circle the wagons" in order to protect themselves from cultural diversity.

Cross-Cultural Relationships

The world is becoming a very small place, and it's amazing how easy it is to change the world if we only get out of our isolationist thinking. We can influence nations just by influencing the people around us. Recently, I attended a conference in Ohio. A prophecy was made to the steering committee of a Christian organization that was present. The person speaking prophetically said that this group was going to touch the nation of Nigeria. After the service a group of Nigerians from the audience approached members of the steering committee. They were able to give firsthand insight to the committee regarding the plans they were about to undertake.

This "small world" presents many wonderful opportunities for Americans. More than 250,000 international students, some of the most intellectual people worldwide, are currently studying at American universities. The children of kings and diplomats, a number of these students are the future leaders of their countries.

Most international students know very little about Christ. One of the things they long for is an American friend. But many of them return to their nations disappointed or embittered at their hosts and with Christianity. One such international student was Isoroku Yamamoto, who became an admiral in the Japanese navy. His experience with prejudice and racism left him extremely bitter. Yamamoto later led the raid on Pearl Harbor.

You don't have to travel abroad to influence the world, but you do have to get over your isolationist thinking and begin to feel the burden for those outside the limits of your personal world.

The Imperial Church

The missionary activities that followed the colonization of nations by the British Empire were also characterized by local thinking. From the late seventeenth century to the mid-twentieth century, British missionaries took the gospel throughout the empire, which extended around the world. For the most part, their mindset was to culturally convert the heathens into proper British ladies and gentlemen, while also converting them to Christ. This was the very mentality held by the first-century Jewish Christians who wanted to make Jews out of the Gentiles before allowing them to become Christians.

Americans have been known for the same approach. We were scheduling a missionary trip to the Amazon a few summers ago. In preparation, I made contact with several Christians in Brazil. During those conversations I learned that Brazilians could always tell when American missionaries had visited a group in their country. They could easily recognize the false concepts of holiness that the Americans would leave. Even when the temperature was above 100 degrees, the missionaries would have the men wearing long pants and the women dressing in skirts down to their ankles.

Perhaps one of the greatest missionary stories of the twentieth century is that of Bruce Olsen. As a nineteen-year-old boy from Minnesota, he bought a one-way ticket to Venezuela and eventually made contact with the Motilone Indians, the fiercest tribe of the Andes and all of South America. After being jabbed through the leg with a six-foot spear upon his first meeting with them, Bruce, or "Bruchko" as they called him, spent three years living among the Motilones, learning the intricacies of their society in order to present the gospel without offending them culturally. Thirty-six years later, Olsen is still there, and the Motilone tribe is 97 percent Christian. Bruce Olsen, in essence, became a Motilone in order to present Christ to them. When he was perceived as one of them, the Motilones were ready to listen.

In 1873, a Belgian Catholic priest named Joseph Damien De Veuster was sent to minister to lepers on the Hawaiian Island of Molokai.

When he arrived, he immediately began to meet each one of the lepers in the colony in hopes of building a friendship. But wherever he turned, people shunned him. It seemed as though every door was closed. He poured his life into his work, erecting a chapel, beginning worship services, and pouring out his heart to the lepers. But it was to no avail. No one responded to his ministry. After twelve years, Father Damien made the decision to leave.

Dejectedly, he made his way to the docks to board a ship to take him back to Belgium. As he stood on the dock, he wrung his hands nervously as he recounted his futile ministry among the lepers. As he did, he looked down at his hand and noticed some mysterious white spots. Immediately, he knew that he had contracted leprosy.

It was then that he knew what he had to do. He returned to the leper colony and to his work. Quickly, the word of his disease spread through the colony. Within a matter of hours, hundreds of lepers gathered outside his hut. They understood his pain, fear, and uncertainty about the future.

The biggest surprise came the following Sunday. As Father Damien arrived at the chapel, he found hundreds of worshippers there. By the time the service began, the chapel was crowded, and many were gathered outside. His ministry became enormously successful because he was one of them. He understood and empathized with them.[5]

Race is not something you can catch. You can't change who you are or where you were born. But identification with others is based on a cultural connection, rather than a racial connection. Without cultural understanding and identification, you'll never be a reconciler. As I mentioned in chapter 7 with regard to the Good Samaritan, love is not a project, and that's what it feels like until people begin to sense they have a common bond with you.

As Christians, we must learn to think globally. That means getting out of our racial isolationism and loving the people God loves—those from "every nation, tribe, and tongue." It also means working very hard to understand and appreciate cultures other than our own.

If the church would engage in this kind of cross-cultural communication, then the gospel could find expression in every culture and ethnic group. What is equally true in America is that if the church would begin to exercise this kind of global thinking, it would automatically begin to model the kind of reconciliation that would restore racial harmony.

RACE AND CULTURE

More than a few missionaries have literally lost their heads upon arrival in a strange land because they did not take time to understand the culture of the people they were imposing their own culture upon. These people won the title of "martyr" only because they lost their lives by offending the people they were sent to help. Some of these mistakes can be blamed on ignorance. But this kind of ignorance often translates as a lack of respect for the indigenous culture. You cannot be an effective reconciler if you view other cultures with an imperial attitude—that is, if you measure all other cultures against the superior standard of your own.

When it comes to racial harmony in our country, the lack of understanding and respect for other cultures can be as big a stumbling block as the color of a person's skin. The easiest way to segregate people is by race. After all, racial diversity is the most obvious form of diversity. Nevertheless, it would be a big mistake to equate race with culture. There are many cultures within the same race, and unfortunately, people of different cultures often don't get along with each other. I know of some Puerto Ricans who hate Mexican people. There are Cubans who hate people from the Dominican Republic. All are Hispanic, but they come from differing cultures and nations. The same kinds of divisions exist among both blacks and whites.

Those who try to establish unity on merely the color of their skin can only achieve a very superficial unity. Finding common ground on a cultural level can quickly overcome racial differences and bind people together—often in more meaningful relationships than those based on the bond of race.

I was on an airplane recently, sitting next to a gentleman who seemed to be working on a series of mathematical equations. Eventually, I asked, "Are you an engineer?"

"Yeah, I'm an engineer," he said. "Mechanical."

"I used to work as a mechanical engineer too," I replied.

"What school did you go to?" he asked.

After we compared engineering information for a few minutes, he started talking about his mother. "My mother used to be a teacher, and in our home, education was stressed."

"Talk about stressing education!" I said. "My mother was also a school teacher, and she used to...."

The conversation took off, and before it ended, I had made a new friend—a friend who was of a different race. We were brought together by a common family culture, which made our racial differences seem insignificant.

The way we relate to people is a lot like the way we relate to God. The Scriptures say that we should walk by what we believe, not by what we see (2 Cor. 5:7). It's easy to come to wrong conclusions about God based on what we see in a given situation. In the same way, walking by sight (skin color) leads to superficial and wrong conclusions.

Everyone looks to build friendships around common interests, concerns, and life situations. Has it ever occurred to you that in any given multiracial situation, the person sharing the most in common with you could be a member of another race? If you only walk by sight, you'll never know. *Prejudice* literally means "to prejudge." In other words, when you're prejudiced, you've predetermined that people of another race share little in common with you culturally. That's why communication with one another is so important. Failing to appreciate other cultures could cost you some of the best relationships of your life.

Sometimes we cannot hear someone else's passion or concern because he or she is different racially or culturally. Throughout this book, I have not disclosed my race so that *all* could hear me and understand the subject of diversity without filtering it through preexisting biases. My role as pastor of a church of more than twenty-five nationalities gives me a platform to teach on the subject of cross-cultural ministry. My testimony, which appears in the first several pages of chapter 5, also gives me a voice as an authentic reconciler. The account of the Jamaican gentleman I called "John" is my personal story. And, it was my family's house that was firebombed. I used the pseudonym "John" to develop trust with my readers based on my understanding of the subject, rather than based on my race.

TRUST: THE ENVIRONMENT OF RECONCILIATION

If you really want to reconcile a relationship, a racially divided church, or an entire nation that has never heard the gospel, you have to foster an environment of trust. The author of Proverbs wrote, *"Trust in the LORD with all your heart and lean not on your own understanding"* (Prov. 3:5). The verse implies that the person who trusts shows an allegiance to God that is based on the heartfelt conviction that the Lord has his or her best interests in mind. The Hebrew word for *trust* is *batach*, which means "to be confident or sure." Its literal meaning suggests an appeal for one to be bold about his or her belief, even to the point of appearing careless. If you want someone of another race to lower his guard and interact with you in a reconciliatory manner, he has to trust you.

Placing your trust in the commonality of *race* rather than *relationship* can be a big mistake because the connection is very superficial. As they say, it's only "skin deep." Considering race as the common denominator of a trust relationship can really backfire on you.

When I was a college student, I took an evening off from classes and went to New York City to do some shopping. At night in New York City, everything imaginable goes on. I was walking down one of the busy streets in Manhattan doing some window-shopping when another black man came up to me.

"Psst! Psst! Hey, brother."

"Yeah, what's up, brother?" I said.

"Come here, man; come here for a second."

Cautiously, I walked a few feet over to where the man was standing. He opened his jacket and pulled out several thick, beautiful gold chains.

"Brother, you gotta help out another brother."

I was still cautious.

"C'mon man; help me out. It's hard out here. You know how it is. The white man's making it hard for us. You see this gold chain? It's twenty-four-karat gold—worth about a hundred dollars. But because you're a brother, I'll sell it to you for twenty-five."

I examined the chain closely, noticing the "24k" engraved on the inside. In my naivete, I said, "All right, I'll take it."

A couple of days later, while taking a shower with the "gold" chain around my neck, I noticed green water draining out of the tub. The "solid gold" chain was really a fake, only coated with the thinnest possible layer of gold. My "brother" had ripped me off. Brotherhood can be pretty superficial, and usually is when it's based only on the color of one's skin.

Transforming the Ideal into Reality

A few years ago, I visited a congregation in Virginia and heard an encouraging story. An all-white church had had a very long and rather dubious heritage of racial prejudice that went back almost one hundred years. A member of the congregation, while working on the history of the church, came across an account in which blacks had been victimized by the racial injustice of the church. That member proposed to her pastor and the governing board that they do something to model reconciliation.

They contacted a large and predominantly black church in the same city and said, "Let's come together and model reconciliation by having an open forum. We need to ask forgiveness for what our forefathers did a hundred years ago. We need to take responsibility and repent of that sin and injustice." Those two congregations came together for a reconciliation service. The whites repented of what their forefathers had done, and the blacks wept and said, "Let's embrace each other as brothers and sisters in Christ." What a powerful time it was!

Now, let's get right down to where we live. It's one thing to agree on the theology of reconciliation and another thing altogether to be a reconciler. *Trust* is a relational word. It's the foundation and the fruit of any sustained dialogue between two groups or individuals. But trust can never truly be trust until it is fleshed out in everyday living.

God's desire is to change us so that we think and feel like Christ, who is the example for us all. Though you may be educated about the evils of prejudice, you may feel emotionally that prejudice is really not so bad. You may believe that God made us all equal, but still feel that your race is really better than other races. The things that you do, the people with whom you associate, and those you befriend are the evidence of what you truly believe in your heart. *"Faith without works is dead,"* wrote the apostle James (James 2:26 NAS). Therefore, not what we say, but what we do is the best measure of prejudice, of racism, and also of a heart that truly desires to follow Christ and be like Him.

———*Chapter 12*———

PULLING DOWN IDOLS AND BUILDING BRIDGES

O ld ideas and attitudes are hard to change. They try to justify their right to the places they hold in your mind simply because they've been around for so long. It's as if bad attitudes take on "intellectual squatters' rights" in your life. Sometimes it's easier to hang on to bad ideas, bad theology, and bad attitudes than it is to change them. The reason more people don't make attitudinal adjustments is because it often feels too difficult, too uncomfortable, or too controversial—not because they don't know their ideas are bad or wrong.

Some may say, "I'm too old to change," as if this were a viable excuse for hanging on to ideas that are outside of God's will. Others say, "My father, my grandfather, and his father before him felt the same way. If it was good enough for them, then it's good enough for me!" The nobility of tradition is lost when it's a bad tradition. Our fathers and forefathers had their own experiences with race relations. And some of them have passed down unbiblical perspectives based on these experiences. Consequently, when we are born again, we come into the kingdom with a lot of baggage. If our forefathers were bigots, racists, victims, or even those who just stood on the sidelines, it doesn't mean we have to be that way.

Walking in a new way doesn't mean that you are betraying your family or your forefathers. But world-class Christians have to reject separatist ideologies, especially when these perceptions are opposed to the cause of Christ. One of the hardest sayings of Jesus had to do with following family versus following Christ.

> [26] *"If anyone comes to Me, and does not hate his own father and mother and wife and children and brothers and sisters, yes, and even his own life, he cannot be My disciple.* [27] *Whoever does not carry his own cross and come after Me cannot be My disciple."* (Luke 14:26–27 NAS)

The cross is an instrument of execution. Just as we must die to self-centeredness in order to be Jesus' disciples, we must also experience the death of many of our attitudes in order to participate in the ministry of reconciliation. Jesus had to die for our sins in order for us to be forgiven and reconciled to God. Unless there is a death, reconciliation can't take place. The misguided ideas you have about people must die. Inappropriate behavior patterns must die. The racial slurs you use at home must die. In order to be reconciled and to function as a minister of reconciliation, a death must first take place.

Reconciling groups with legacies of prejudice and injustice requires that the multiethnic church tear down the mental idols that have been perpetuated throughout generations. Bitterness, prejudice, and other by-products of racial tension are the idols of racism. When we think of an idol, we usually picture a statue, with people bowing down before it. But idols can also be ideas and beliefs to which people render obedience and devotion.

Modern-day idols are usually those of the heart and mind. I've never known anyone who actually bowed down to worship in a bank.

Nevertheless, money and materialism are indeed idols in our culture. These idols are even referred to in Scripture:

> *Therefore consider the members of your earthly body as dead to immorality, impurity, passion, evil desire, and greed, which amounts to idolatry.* (Col. 3:5 NAS)

The presence of an idol in our lives offends a wholly righteous and just God. Such an idol must be pulled down.

GRAVEN IMAGES

People often harbor false images because they simply don't know any better; it's all they've been taught. But true reconcilers will never settle for false or unbiblical models of reconciliation, of the church, or even of Jesus Christ Himself. If I build a church with a black Jesus portrayed in a stained-glass window, is that a biblical model? The answer is both yes and no.

While Jesus is the Christ for Africans and African-Americans, in order to have an appropriate model of Christ, I would need to have a stained-glass window with a Caucasian Jesus, an Asian Jesus, an Indian Jesus, and so on. I don't have enough windows to reflect the heart of God for the nations! Even if I did, someone would then want a tall Jesus, a short Jesus, an athletic Jesus, or a fly-fishing Jesus. A fly-fishing Jesus might seem ridiculous, but so is the need to have a Savior with the same skin pigmentation as your own.

I am aware of the fact that Jesus was a Jew, born in Palestine. He was not an Asian, an African, or an Indian. I also know that He was not a fair-haired, blue-eyed Anglo-Saxon as He is often portrayed. If that's your mental picture of Jesus, you need to tear it down; it's a faulty image. Paul wrote to the Corinthians about pulling down false images:

> [4]*(For the weapons of our warfare are not carnal, but mighty*
> *through God to the pulling down of strong holds;)* [5]*Casting*
> *down imaginations, and every high thing that exalteth itself*
> *against the [true] knowledge of God, and bringing into cap-*
> *tivity every thought to the obedience of Christ....*
>
> (2 Cor. 10:4–5 KJV)

The Bible doesn't tell us what Jesus looked like—thank God! If we had a photograph of Jesus, the likelihood is that people would eventually resort to worshipping the earthly image rather than the eternal Son of God. For this reason, the second of the Ten Commandments is that we're to make no graven image of things in heaven (Deut. 5:8–9). Unfortunately, some people have become so race conscious that they have to have a Jesus of their own making before they will follow Him— a black Jesus, a Chinese Jesus, or a Latino Jesus.

I have had several opportunities to talk with Black Muslims. The first question they ask when I present Christ as Savior is, *"What color was Jesus?"* I usually answer with another question: "What color is your sin?"

"Sin has no color," they reply.

"And neither does its sacrifice," I say.

Jesus was a Middle-Eastern Semite. Nevertheless, He identifies with all people of every race. John Gilman, president of Dayspring International, has a unique way of presenting the story of Jesus Christ to people in India. *Daya Sakar* ("Oceans of Mercy") is a film portraying the life of Christ with all Indian actors. Some of the Dayspring missionaries carry projectors and generators on horseback, venturing into the most remote parts of the country to show *Daya Sakar* on bed sheets strung up between trees. The response to the film and to the gospel has been almost unbelievable. In some cases, a single copy of the film has been shown fifteen hundred times. Dayspring International is also producing a film on the life of Christ using all African actors.

There are many who would be offended or even outraged if they saw John Gilman's film featuring a black Jesus rather than a white actor. That is an idol that needs to be pulled down. Some Black Muslims have rejected Jesus, saying that He cannot be their Savior since He was not black. That, too, is an idol of racism.

The reason idolatry is such an offense to God is that it represents worship of the creation as if it were the Creator. You have to be pretty committed to "ignorance" (i.e., the habit of ignoring self-evident truth) to worship a statue. In the same way, subjugating spiritual truth to skin color is equally absurd.

Films like *Daya Sakar* are so effective because they say to the Indians that Jesus died for them too. One who is infected with racist idolatry elevates the race factor and makes it the primary means of identification. The Black Muslims, as well as those who follow a mixture of Christianity and Nazi doctrine, serve racial idols. They will only follow Christ if He died for their race alone. Anglo-Saxons don't "own" Jesus any more than the Jews do. The point is that He came to identify with every man. If that's not your image of Jesus, tear it down!

THE PROPHETIC NATURE OF RECONCILIATION

Words and deeds are the best indications of what is truly in the heart. Do you really believe in reconciliation? If you do, you'll stand up for it; if you don't, you won't. You must be willing to confront someone else on the issue, not just because they are sinning, but because as they're sinning, they are injuring other people and treating them unjustly.

There is a prophetic nature to the ministry of reconciliation. The Old Testament prophets had a two-fold ministry: 1) to tell and foretell the purpose of God; and, 2) to confront sin and injustice. Reconcilers are prophetic because the root cause of prejudice and racism is not merely a misunderstanding. There are issues of right and wrong for which someone needs to take a stand.

A prophet, especially a prophet in the spirit of those in the Old Testament, cannot tolerate hypocrisy or injustice. The prophet cries out against unrighteousness and injustice. Unfortunately, many Evangelicals today label people who promulgate any semblance of social conscious-ness as "liberals" or "leftist radicals." But the categorical demand for social justice follows the tradition of Elijah, Isaiah, Jeremiah, John the Baptist, and Jesus Himself.

Modern Evangelicals have so concentrated on preaching the mes-sage of salvation that the responsibility to work for social change has been virtually abandoned. One reason for this is because some Evangelicals think of the church as a place to escape from the world. They think they should have as little involvement as possible with what's going on beyond the walls of the church. Others are so caught up with the fact that the Lord Jesus might return any minute that they see no reason to "polish the brass on a sinking ship." Still others are so preoc-cupied with the doctrines of God's sovereignty and man's predestina-tion that they think that everything is the way God wants it to be.

Whatever the reason, modern Evangelicals often disassociate themselves from the responsibility of addressing social problems in-side and outside of the church. Historically, the Evangelical church has led the way in confronting social sin and injustice. One outstanding example is the Clapham Parish Church in early nineteenth-century England. William Wilberforce, a member of Parliament who had con-verted to Christianity, along with Lord Shaftesbury, led a long, arduous assault on the British slave-trading industry. After his conversion, Wilberforce had been inspired to action by none other than John Newton, the converted slave trader who wrote the hymn "Amazing Grace."

Christians who had been touched by the English Awakening rallied behind Wilberforce. The Clapham Parish leaders met together daily in hours of prayer for success. Christians all over the nation commonly held long prayer meetings on the eve of every critical debate in parliament where Wilberforce and Shaftesbury would speak of the intolerable issue of racial injustice. Christians ceaselessly published materials on the evils of slavery, gathered petitions from all over the nation, and boycotted goods produced by slaves. The church was, at this moment in history, fulfilling its prophetic mission to speak out against injustice and to pull down idols.

In 1807, a bill abolishing the slave trade was passed by a vote of 283 to 16, with an overwhelming acclamation for Wilberforce. In 1833, British slave owners were ordered to release their slaves in a year's time and were compensated with a gift of twenty million pounds from the English treasury. Historian W. E. Lechy called it "one of the three or four totally righteous acts of government in history."[1] It is inconceivable that such a work could have been accomplished without a nation of evangelical Christians, revived by the English Awakening.

There was a corresponding revival in America, known today as the Second Great Awakening. Preachers such as Charles Finney and Lyman Beecher called men to repentance and salvation. They also decried the evils of slavery.

But as phenomenal as the revival fires were regarding conversions, the idols of racism had been firmly established over many generations. Many Christians, particularly those in the South, were far too timid about pulling down the idols of their forefathers. For the most part, they manipulated their theology to accommodate their racial idolatry. Because the church (that is, the Christians) did not eradicate slavery, it was done away with by the judgment of God—a judgment that cost America six hundred thousand lives. Even after that enormous loss, in many ways we are still lacking full reconciliation to this day.

Herbert Schlossberg wrote a powerful, thought-provoking book about the ideological idols that exist in American culture. In *Idols for Destruction,* he contrasts the secular and biblical ways of looking at history.

> Edward Gibbon's history of Rome made spatial analogies—such as rise, decline, fall—commonplace in evaluating civilizations. In the twentieth century, organic phrases perhaps have become more common....Societies are thought of as being born, growing, decaying, dying. Other terms are sometimes drawn from social sciences or from the requirements of political propaganda. Thus, a society may be said to be coming of age, to be attaining self-consciousness, to be throwing off the chains of oppression, to be entering the dark age, to be entering a golden age.[2]

Schlossberg continues, showing that God has a different set of words and a different perception about the beginning and end of a society.

> Spatial and biological analogies are incompatible with biblical thinking....In place of these analogies the biblical explanation of the end of a society uses the concept of judgment....[Israel's] rebellion against God was accompanied by a turning to idolatry, and this idolatry brought the nation to its end. "With their silver and gold," said the prophet Hosea, "they made idols for their own destruction" (Hosea 8:4).[3]

Judgment—even judgment against nations in the Old Testament—rarely comes in the form of a supernatural manifestation. Often God allows nations to be defeated as a consequence of their sin and idolatry. Abraham Lincoln understood that the Civil War wasn't merely the result of political and economic differences, but was judgment from God because the nation did not rid itself of the sin of racial injustice. Though the institution of slavery has long since been abolished, the same kind of racial idolatry continues to abide within many people. If the church refuses to deal with it, the resulting chaos and social fragmentation will result in God's judgment on a society that refuses to pull down the idols of prejudice and racism.

PULLING DOWN IDOLS

The Old Testament book of Judges contains the familiar account of Gideon. The angel of the Lord appeared to Gideon and called him to deliver Israel from the domination of the Midianites. In order to confirm the angel's message, Gideon twice put out a fleece; on one morning it was wet while the ground around it was dry, and on another it was dry while the ground was wet.

After the Lord reduced Gideon's army to only a few hundred men, they surrounded the Midian camp. That night, each man carried a torch inside an earthen jar and a trumpet. At the signal, the jars were broken, and the small band of men blew their trumpets. In the confusion that followed, Gideon's small army defeated the Midianites and established peace in Israel—peace that lasted forty years.

The Lord had tested the thirty-two thousand that had initially comprised Gideon's army until the force numbered only three hundred. But there is an important part of the story that is often overlooked. Immediately after the angel called him, Gideon himself was tested.

25Now the same night it came about that the LORD said to him, "Take your father's bull and a second bull seven years old, and pull down the altar of Baal which belongs to your father, and cut down the Asherah that is beside it; 26and build an altar to the LORD your God on the top of this stronghold in an orderly manner, and take a second bull and offer a burnt offering with the wood of the Asherah which you shall cut down."

27Then Gideon took ten men of his servants and did as the LORD had spoken to him; and it came about, because he was too afraid of his father's household and the men of the city to do it by day, that he did it by night.

(Judg. 6:25–27 NAS)

Both the altar of Baal and the Asherah were household idols worshipped by Gideon's family and their servants. In order to be a deliverer or a reconciler, the first thing many people will have to do is to pull down the mental idols and false images that their families have worshipped and passed down to them. Unfortunately, people who are called of God to come into His house to worship often drag in the idols they inherited from their forefathers.

Before you or I can bring an acceptable sacrifice, we have to do some house cleaning. You cannot continue to harbor hatred, prejudice, or bitterness, regardless of whether your forefathers were slaves or slaveowners. You can no longer laugh at the racial jokes, give approval to others' racism by your tacit consent, or share sentiments that spring out of old bitterness. To be a prophetic reconciler, you'll have to start pulling down some idols—first your father's bull, then your own, then the others you'll run into along the way.

It's not unusual to be afraid of the repercussions that often accompany the pulling down of idols. But you're in good company. Gideon felt the same way. He wasn't strong enough to follow the Lord's command in broad daylight, so he did the deed at night. At first, you may not be able to stand up courageously against the prejudicial and racist attitudes around you. But you can refuse to participate. You can deal with the attitudes in your own heart. You can be a model of reconciliation in your personal friendships. You can be an example in offering the regular acts of kindness that go a long way toward bridging the gap that is dividing both the church and our nation. The best way to get to a new place is to take a step in that direction. Eventually you will be surprised to discover that even small steps can have enormous effects on the people around you. Soon you'll look back and discover that God has enabled you to develop a multicultural lifestyle.

End Notes

Introduction

1. Don Eberly, *Restoring the Good Society* (Grand Rapids: Baker Book House, 1994), 23.
2. S. D. Gaede, *When Tolerance Is No Virtue* (Downers Grove, Ill.: InterVarsity Press, 1993), 21.
3. Cal Thomas and Edward Dobson, *Blinded By Might* (Grand Rapids: Zondervan Publishing House, 1999), 80.
4. "One Lord, One Faith, One Voice," *Christianity Today*, October 1996, 38.

Chapter 2: Diversity: The Nature of the Kingdom

1. Flavil Yeakley, *Why Churches Grow* (Arvada, Colo.: Christian Communications, 1979), 65.
2. Rick Warren, *The Purpose Driven Church* (Grand Rapids: Zondervan Publishing House, 1995), 157.
3. Robert E. Webber, *The Church in the World* (Grand Rapids: Academie Books, 1986), 31.
4. To obtain C. Peter Wagner's *Gift Profile Test*, contact The Charles E. Fuller Institute, Pasadena, Calif.
5. Mortimer B. Zuckerman, "Louis Farrakhan's White Noise," *U.S. News and World Report*, 6 November 1995, 96.
6. Timothy C. Morgan and Tom Giles, "Simpson Verdict, Farrakhan March Energize Interracial Dialogue," *Christianity Today*, 13 November 1995, 78.

7. Charles H. Spurgeon, *The Treasury of David* (Peabody, Mass.: Hendrickson Publishers), Vol. 3:169.

8. Merrill F. Unger, *The New Unger's Bible Dictionary* (Chicago: Moody Press, 1988), 555.

Chapter 3: The Multiethnic Church

1. Ray Bakke, *A Theology as Big as the City* (Downers Grove, Ill.: InterVarsity Press, 1997), 13.

2. Ibid., 12.

3. Michael Green, *Evangelism in the Early Church* (Grand Rapids: Eerdmans Publishing Company, 1970), 113.

4. *Harper's Bible Dictionary* (New York: Harper and Row, 1985), 33.

5. Green, *Evangelism in the Early Church*, 114.

6. F. F. Bruce, *The New International Commentary on the New Testament, The Book of Acts* (Grand Rapids: Eerdmans Publishing Company, 1986), 101.

7. G. W. Bromley, gen. ed., *The International Standard Bible Encyclopedia* (Grand Rapids: Eerdmans Publishing Company, 1979), 1:843.

8. Thom Hopler, *A World of Difference* (Downers Grove, Ill.: InterVarsity Press, 1981), 109.

9. Bruce, *New International Commentary*, 245.

10. Robert Kelley, *The Power of Followership* (New York: Doubleday Currency, 1992), 37.

11. James S. Hewitt, ed., *Illustrations Unlimited* (Wheaton: Tyndale House Publishers, 1988), 391.

12. Ibid.

13. Ibid., 19.

End Notes

Chapter 5: Looking in the Mirror

1. Paul Cedar, Kent Hughes, and Ben Patterson, *Mastering the Pastoral Role* (Portland: Multnomah Press, 1991), 28.
2. John R. W. Stott, *Between Two Worlds* (Grand Rapids: Eerdmans Publishing Company, 1982), 138.
3. George Barna, *Today's Pastors* (Ventura: Regal Books, 1993), 44.
4. Ron Marsico, "Bias Crime Victims Gain Right To Sue Criminals for Damages," *The Essex County (N.J.) Star Ledger*, 12 June 1993, 7.
5. Ibid.
6. "L. A. Riot," *U.S. News and World Report*, 31 May 1993, 36.
7. David Claerbaut, *Urban Ministry* (Grand Rapids: Zondervan Publishing House, 1983), 130.
8. "The 21st Century Seminary," *Christianity Today*, 17 May 1993, 45–46.

Chapter 6: Are You Comfortable Around Me?

1. *Random House College Dictionary*, revised edition, s.v. "prejudice."
2. *Webster's Ninth New Collegiate Dictionary*, s.v. "prejudice."
3. *The New English Dictionary*, s.v. "prejudice."
4. Gordon W. Allport, *The Nature of Prejudice* (New York: Addison-Wesley Publishing Company, 1979), 9.
5. Ibid.
6. Raleigh Washington and Glenn Kehrein, *Breaking Down Walls* (Chicago: Moody Press, 1993), 13–14.
7. Allport, *Nature of Prejudice*, 14–15.
8. Kenneth B. Clark, *Prejudice and Your Child* (Boston: Beacon Press, 1964), 27.
9. F. F. Bruce, *New Testament History* (New York: Doubleday Dell Publishing, 1969), 236.

Chapter 7: Who Is My Neighbor?

1. Herbert Lockyer, Sr., gen. ed., *Nelson's Illustrated Bible Dictionary* (Nashville: Thomas Nelson Publishers, 1986), 941–43.
2. Joachim Jeremias, *The Parables of Jesus* (Upper Saddle River, N.J.: Prentice-Hall, 1972), 203.
3. Norval Geldenhuys, *Commentary on the Gospel of Luke* (London: Marshall, Morgan and Scott, 1965), 313.
4. Don Stephens, *Mandate for Mercy* (Seattle: YWAM Publishing, 1995), 20.

Chapter 8: The Initiative of Reconciliation

1. Herman Ridderbos, *Paul: An Outline of His Theology* (Grand Rapids: Eerdmans Publishing Company, 1975), 183.
2. Ibid., 182.
3. Archibald Thomas Robinson, *Word Pictures in the New Testament* (Grand Rapids: Baker Book House, 1931), 232.
4. Cecil B. Murphey, *Dictionary of Biblical Literacy* (Nashville: Thomas Nelson Publishers, 1989), 557.
5. Philip E. Hughes, *The New International Commentary on the New Testament, the Second Epistle to the Corinthians* (Grand Rapids: Eerdmans Publishing Company, 1962), 204.
6. Kenneth W. Osbeck, *101 Hymn Stories* (Grand Rapids: Kregel Publications, 1982), 28.

Chapter 9: Creating an Expression of Kingdom Diversity

1. Cyril C. Richardson, ed., *Early Church Fathers* (New York: Macmillan Publishing Co., Inc., 1976), 88.

Chapter 10: Cross-Cultural Worship

1. Barna, *Today's Pastors*, 44.
2. Robert E. Webber, *Worship Old and New* (Grand Rapids: Zondervan Publishing House, 1982), 98.
3. John E. Burkhart, *Worship* (Philadelphia: The Westminster Press, 1982), 17.
4. Judson Cornwall, *Worship As David Lived It* (Shippensburg, Pa.: Revival Press, 1990), 8.
5. James E. Bordwine, *A Guide to the Westminster Standards* (Jefferson, Md., The Trinity Foundation, 1991), xv.
6. H. Richard Niebuhr, *Christ and Culture* (New York: Harper Torchbooks, 1951), 33.
7. C. Peter Wagner, ed., *Church Growth: The State of the Art* (Wheaton: Tyndale House Publishers, 1986), 53.
8. Philip Keller, *A Shepherd Looks at Psalm 23* (New York: Harper Paperbacks, 1970), 63–64.
9. Robert E. Webber, *Worship Is a Verb* (Peabody, Mass.: Hendrickson Publishers, 1992), 130.

Chapter 11: Cross-Cultural Relationships

1. Bureau of the Census, U. S. Department of Commerce.
2. "I Am Who I Am," *Time*, 5 May 1997, 33–34.
3. Tara Franklin, personal communication with author, Montclair, N.J., 15 January 1998.
4. Sherwood G. Lingenfelter and Marvin K. Mayers, *Ministering Cross-Culturally* (Grand Rapids: Baker Book House, 1986), 74.
5. Hewitt, *Illustrations Unlimited*, 327.

Chapter 12: Pulling Down Idols and Building Bridges

1. Richard Lovelace, *Dynamics of Spiritual Life* (Downers Grove, Ill.: InterVarsity Press, 1979), 369–70.
2. Herbert Schlossberg, *Idols for Destruction* (Wheaton: Crossway Books, 1990), 4.
3. Ibid., 6.

Subject Index

A

Aaron, 71, 99

Abraham, 109

Accommodation, 158, 176

Acts, Book of, 41, 48, 53, 60, 61, 67, 68, 100, 150

Adam, 67, 70, 71, 99

African-American, 16, 25, 34, 46, 78, 82, 90, 115, 138, 143, 144, 158, 178, 195

Afro-centric, 21

Allport, Dr. Gordon, 94-95, 97

Amazing Grace, 129, 135, 199

Anglo-centric, 21

Antioch, 47-48, 50, 52, 54, 56, 58, 61

Apartheid, 25, 75, 180

Arab, 132

Asians, 76, 82, 96, 153, 158, 171, 181, 195

B

Bakke, Ray, 45-46

Ballou, Earle, H., 58

Bangladesh, 114

Baptists, 144

Barna, George (Research Group), 84-85

Barnabas, 51-53, 62

Beecher, Lyman, 199

Begin, Menachem, 132

Belgium, 185

Bi-cultural, 52

Bigotry, 95

Bi-racial, 178, 179

Black Muslims, 91-92

Boomers ("Baby"), 168

Booth, William, 61

Browning of America, 173, 179

Bruce, F. F., 51, 54, 102

Burkhart, John, 155

Busters ("Baby"), 168

C

Caucasians, 35, 82, 90, 92, 97, 173, 181, 195

Chariots of Fire, 63

Cho, David Yongii, 33

Christ Church, 17, 21, 25, 43, 45, 56, 83, 135, 138-139, 143, 146, 151, 168-169, 177, 181

ALSO BY DAVID IRELAND

Failure Is Written In Pencil

Failure has a way of cutting to the core of your being leaving you emotionally dejected. Like a dreaded virus wreaking havoc in the body's bloodstream, failure attacks the immune system of the soul. David Ireland presents a healing prescription to the crippling ravages of failure using his captivating motivational style. You will find yourself laughing, crying, and identifying with notable men and women who have come to understand that *Failure Is Written in Pencil*—it's erasable.

ISBN: 0-9627907-3-7
$13.00 — soft cover; over 180 pages

Activating the Gifts of the Holy Spirit

God wants the gifts He has given you to become evident in every area of your life. In this dynamic book, David Ireland shows how you can activate the power of the Holy Spirit in your daily walk with God. Discover how you can...

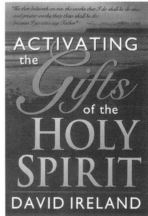

- Understand the gifts of the Spirit
- Hear the voice of the Holy Spirit
- Know God's heart in every spiritual matter
- Be miraculously used by God
- Take authority over Satan's tricks and deceptions...and more!

ISBN: 0-88368-484-5
$11.00 — soft cover; 175 pages

Life-Changing Messages Available on Cassette

6 Habits of World-Class Leaders

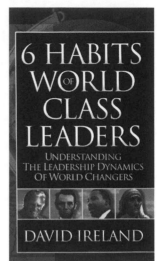

In a rapidly changing world, there is a pressing need for effective leaders. Through this vital, motivational tool, David Ireland describes the habits of world–class leaders and how they use these tools to remain effective in their areas of influence. Through this six-cassette album you will learn such essential leadership skills as:

- Failure Gives You an Edge
- How to Develop the Leader Within
- The Importance of Mentoring
- Problem-Solving…and more!

6-Cassettes — $30.00

Understanding Dreams

Throughout the ages, the subject of dreams has mystified scientists and baffled the common man. Yet almost everyone dreams. The Bible proves that these night visions are often used by God to communicate to people in a unique and unobstructed way. Through this revealing three-tape series, Pastor Ireland demystifies the ethereal realm of dreams and shows you how they can provide direction for your life through this provocative, in-depth study.

3-Cassettes — $15.00

Life-Changing Messages Available on Cassette

Becoming a World Changer

Every person can effect change in his or her sphere of influence. World
changes continually model God's inclusive integrity by reconciling themselves to others of different racial, ethnic, and cultural backgrounds. These courageous men and women refuse to be deterred from their goal to see racial divisions come down. World changers recognize that the reconciliation of man to God is incomplete without the adjoining reconciliation of man to man. Through this dynamic series on three cassettes David Ireland challenges you to reshape your world to enhance the glorious mosaic of God, one life at a time.

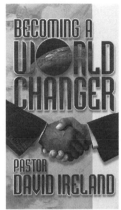

3-Cassettes — $15.00

Home Improvement

In this provocative family series, Pastor David Ireland
presents six practical messages outlining practical, biblical principles that will help you strengthen the relationships that mean the most to you. This essential cassette series addresses such complex family issues as:

- Building an Affair-Proof Marriage
- The Blended Family
- Single and Satisfied
- What I Wish My Parents Knew

6-Cassettes — $30.00

Life-Changing Messages Available on Cassette

Avoiding Sexual Pitfalls

Judging from today's talk shows, multitudes of men, women, and children have fallen into the disillusioning trap of sexual perversion. In this healing and candid three-tape series, Pastor Ireland exposes the unforeseen pitfalls of sexual sins. Through these messages, he teaches that God never intended sex to be used as a lethal weapon or as a deceptive lure. Rather, God created sex for our procreation and for our pleasure. Learn to put healthy boundaries around your sexual behavior through these practical messages.

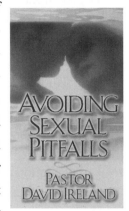

3-Cassettes — $15.00

Healing Victims of Abuse

This dynamic series offers therapeutic comfort to victims and victimizers of physical, sexual, and spiritual abuse in three cassettes. David Ireland uses his unique expository preaching style to build a bridge of trust for the hurting. In this life-transforming series, our teacher outlines the stages of emotional suffering and maps out a plan that moves the listeners from pain to peace.

3-Cassettes — $15.00

Life-Changing Messages Available on Cassette

The Ministry of Reconciliation

The ministry of reconciliation transcends the mere act of soul winning. The church has the additional responsibility 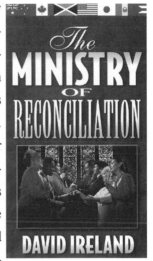 to reflect God's restorative nature in producing social harmony based on forgiveness, acceptance, and love of all people. It has been said that 11:00 a.m. on Sunday mornings is the most racially segregated hour in America. This statement leads us to conclude that our theology is sullied by separatism and ethnocentrism. Through this three-cassette series you will discover how God seeks to elevate His church to a place where it embraces and celebrates people of all races, cultures and nationalities.

3-Cassettes — $15.00

To order these resources visit our on-line bookstore at www.impactminstry.org. You may also use our convenient Order Form on the last page or call **1-800-850-6522** for credit card orders.

Order Form
(You may photocopy this form)

	Qty.	Price	Total

BOOKS:

	Qty.	Price	Total
What Color Is Your God?	_____	$13.00	_____
Failure Is Written In Pencil	_____	$13.00	_____
Activating The Gifts of The Holy Spirit	_____	$11.00	_____

CASSETTE ALBUMS:

	Qty.	Price	Total
6 Habits of World Class Leaders	_____	$30.00	_____
Understanding Dreams	_____	$15.00	_____
Becoming A World Changer	_____	$15.00	_____
Home Improvement	_____	$30.00	_____
Avoiding Sexual Pitfalls	_____	$15.00	_____
Healing Victims of Abuse	_____	$15.00	_____
The Ministry of Reconciliation	_____	$15.00	_____

Subtotal _____

Postage & Handling:
- • Add 10% of Order (minimum of $2.00) _____
- • (Orders outside the U.S. add 20%) _____
- • New Jersey residents add 6% Sales Tax _____

Total Enclosed (U.S. funds only) _____

Send payment with order to:

IMPACT Publishing House
96 Pompton Ave.
Verona, NJ 07044

For quantity discounts or credit card orders, call:
1-800-850-6522

Name: _____

Address: _____

City: _____ State: _____ Zip: _____

Country: _____

For additional ministry resources from David Ireland visit our online bookstore at: **www.impactministry.org.**